Learn C
in Three Days

Sam A. Abolrous

Wordware Publishing, Inc.

Library of Congress Cataloging-in-Publication Data

Abolrous, Sam A.
  Learn C in three days / Sam A. Abolrous.
    p. cm.
  Includes index.
  ISBN 1-55622-298-X
  1. C (Computer program language).   I. Title.
QA76.73.C15A22   1992
005.13'3--dc20   92-11346
                                                  CIP

ISBN1-55622-298-X

10 9 8 7 6 5 4 3 2 1

9206

The examples and programs contained in this book are compatible with the
ANSI standard, Microsoft C, Quick C, Turbo C++, Power C and many others.
The programs in this book were compiled using Turbo C++ and tested for
compatibility on Quick C and Power C.

Microsoft C and Quick C are trademarks of Microsoft Corporation.
Turbo C and Turbo C++ are trademarks of Borland International.
Power C is a trademark of Mix Software, Inc.
Other product names mentioned are used for identification purposes only and may be
trademarks of their respective companies.

All inquiries for volume purchases of this book should be addressed to
Wordware Publishing, Inc., at the above address. Telephone inquiries may be
made by calling:

(214) 423-0090

Contents

Preface

"Is it possible to **Learn C in three days**?" The answer is YES.

Without too much hassle with types of identifiers, pointers, and constants, this book will take you to the heart of the **C** programming language through step-by-step examples, giving you experience in **C** in a small amount of time.

You start with simple programs which crunch some numbers and print some strings, and you end up with useful applications of data structures and files. The examples contained in this book are carefully chosen to show you the pitfalls that you may face in creating your own programs.

The second question is: "Which **C** am I going to learn?"

You know that there are many dialects of **C** around, such as **Turbo C, Quick C, Power C**, and the extensions of **C++,** and so forth. The original **C** language was introduced by Brian Kernighan and Dennis Ritchie (**K&R**) in their book *The C Programming Language* (Prentice-Hall, 1978), then the proposed **ANSI** standard introduced an expanded version of the language. The different versions of the languages are nonportable in some areas (such as graphics), but you can still write a portable program that compiles and runs using any compiler. This is the main feature of this book. Whatever compiler you use, the programs will still compile and run.

Sam A. Abolrous

DAY ONE

Chapter One

YOUR FIRST TOUR OF C

1-1 THE C PROGRAM

In order to see what the structure of a **C** program looks like, it is best to start with a simple program. Figure 1-1 shows a program that displays on the screen the message "Hi there."

```
/*   Figure 1-1      */
#include <stdio.h>
main()
{
    printf("Hi there");
}
```

The heart of this program is the *function* **printf,** which actually does the work here. As a matter of fact, the **C** language is built from functions (like **printf**) that execute different tasks. The function(s), however, must be used inside a framework which starts with the word **main( ),** followed by the *block* containing the function(s) which is marked by the braces ({ }).

The first line starting with the characters **/*** and ending with the characters ***/** is a *comment.* You may type as many lines as you wish between these two sets of characters and the compiler will ignore them as being comments. Comments can appear anywhere in the program.

The second line that starts with **#include** is called a *directive.* It is not a part of the actual program. It is used as a command to the compiler to direct the translation of the program. There are other directives which must be used according to the type of functions used in the main block, but this specific directive appears in all programs as it refers to the *standard input output header* file (**stdio.h**). Many compilers may compile this simple program successfully without the directive, but it is a good habit to include this directive at the beginning of any **C** program. When using more than one directive each must appear on a single line.

Blank lines and spaces inside the program are optional except the blank space following the directives and similar keywords.

The function **printf** is embedded into a *statement* whose ending is marked by the semicolon (;). This is important syntax of the C program because the semicolon tells the compiler that a statement is finished.

As is clear from Figure 1-1, all C programs are written in lowercase letters.

1-2 DISPLAYING TEXT

The **printf** is the most important function used to display text on the screen. Like any function it has two parentheses, between which comes the *string* to be displayed, enclosed in quotations. Look at the output of the program shown in Figure 1-2. It uses two successive statements using the **printf** function.

NOTE
A companion diskette comes along with this book to help you save time and effort. This diskette contains the source code of all the examples, in addition to the solutions to the drills. You can either compile them directly or use them for comparison and error checking. Please read the "readme" file on the distribution disk. Just type the command **README** and press **Enter**.

```
/*   Figure 1-2    */
#include <stdio.h>
main()
{
    printf("Hi there");
    printf("How are you today?");
}
```

If you compile this program and run it, the displayed output is:

```
Hi thereHow are you today?
```

Just like that.

In order to have the output displayed on two separate lines you must add the *new-line character* (\n) at the end of the first string, as shown in Figure 1-3.

```
/*   Figure 1-3    */
#include <stdio.h>
main()
{
    printf("Hi there\n");
    printf("How are you today?");
}
```

Now the output is:

```
Hi there
How are you today?
```

It is clear that the new-line character (**\n**) comes right after the string and must be inside the quotation marks. Each **\n** corresponds to a new line, so you can skip another line by using **\n\n** at the end of the first string.

Actually, any spaces or characters written between the quotations, unless they have a special meaning, will be displayed as a part of the text. Figure 1-4 demonstrates how to join two strings with a blank space between them.

```
/*   Figure 1-4    */
#include <stdio.h>
main()
{
    printf("Hi there, ");
    printf("how are you today?");
}
```

The output of this program is:

```
Hi there, how are you today?
```

This way you can design a label for yourself, by writing a small program like the one shown in Figure 1-5.

```
/*   Figure 1-5    */
#include <stdio.h>
main()
{
    printf("WORDWARE PUBLISHING, INC.\n");
    printf("--------------------------\n");
    printf("1506 CAPITAL AVENUE\n");
    printf("PLANO, TEXAS 75074\n");
}
```

This program displays on the screen the following text:

```
WORDWARE PUBLISHING, INC.
--------------------------
1506 CAPITAL AVENUE
PLANO, TEXAS 75074
```

More about the **printf** function later.

1-3 CRUNCHING NUMBERS

When dealing with numbers you have to pay attention to the type of each number, whether **float, int**eger, etc. Each type has to be used with the **printf** function in a specific format. The example in Figure 1-6 displays the two numbers 128 and 128.0. The first is of the type **int** while the second is of the type **float**. Notice two new characters inside the quotation marks, **%d** (which stands for "decimal"), and **%f** (which stands for "float"). The number itself appears outside the quotation marks, preceded by a comma.

```
/*      Figure 1-6      */
#include <stdio.h>
main()
{
        printf("%d\n",128);
        printf("%f\n",128.0);
}
```

The characters **%d** and **%f** are called *conversion specifiers*. In this program, they are used to tell the compiler about the types of numbers appearing in the program, which in turn determine the suitable memory storage locations. They are referred to also as *format characters* or *format specifiers*. They have other properties that are discussed later.

Executing this program displays the following:

```
128
128.000000
```

What if you used the wrong conversion specifiers? Try that by swapping the **%d** and the **%f** as shown in Figure 1-7.

```
/*   Figure 1-7    */
#include <stdio.h>
main()
{
    printf("%f\n",128);
    printf("%d\n",128.0);
}
```

The output from this program is:

```
0.000000
0
```

Wrong results!

Some compilers, however, will give unpredictable results by dumping some garbage numbers in the output.

The **printf** can also handle mathematical expressions which are evaluated and displayed. Figure 1-8 shows an example of such simple mathematical expressions. The first one (128*2) is multiplication, and the second (128.0/2) is division.

```
/*   Figure 1-8     */
#include <stdio.h>
main()
{
    printf("%d\n",128*2);
    printf("%f\n",128.0/2);
}
```

The output from this program is:

```
256
64.000000
```

Did you notice that we used the integer 2 in the division? It is possible to use mixed types and still get a float output, but it is recommended to use the same type of numbers in the expression.

1-4 USING VARIABLES

Variables are actually memory locations, but programmers refer to them by names because it is easier than referring to them by addresses. In **C**, there are not as many restrictions on naming variables as with other languages. Some names are reserved for the compiler (such as **int** and **main**) because they have special meanings. The user-invented names of the variables are called *identifiers*. They may be composed of letters (a-z or A-Z), digits (0-9), or underscores (_), with the first character being a letter or an underscore. A good feature of the **C** identifiers is that they may be very long, which allows for descriptive names like:

    The_total_number_of_cars_sold_year_to_date
    The_total_direct_cost_for_12_months_budget_period

If the identifier is longer than 32 characters, only the first 32 characters are significant.

While both uppercase and lowercase letters are accepted as identifiers, they are not equivalent. In other words, the variable "PRICE" is not the same as the variable "price."

DECLARING VARIABLES The most important restriction on using variables is that they have to be declared at the beginning of the program. For example:

```
/*   Figure 1-9     */
#include <stdio.h>
main( )
{
/* Declarations */
     int a;
     float b;
/* Display output */
     printf("%d\n",a);
     printf("%f\n",b);
}
```

As you can see in Figure 1-9, the declarations come at the beginning. Two variables are declared, "a" as an **int**eger, and "b" as a **float**. The next part of the program displays the values stored in the variables using the suitable conversion specifiers. No values are really stored in the variables so far, so you should expect the output to be something like:

```
7212
0.000000
```

The first value is nothing but what was there in the memory location. In other words, variables which are not initialized or assigned values may contain garbage.

ASSIGNMENT   In the next step we assign values to these variables. See Figure 1-10.

```
/*   Figure 1-10    */
#include <stdio.h>
main( )
{
/* Declarations */
     int a;
     float b;
/* Assignment */
     a=1024;
     b=512;
/* Display output */
     printf("%d\n",a);
     printf("%f\n",b);
}
```

Now the program contains one more part, where the value 1024 is assigned to the variable "a," and the value 512 is assigned to the variable "b."

This program gives the result:

```
1024
512.000000
```

You also can assign variables (or expressions containing variables) to other variables as in the following example, Figure 1-11.

```
/*    Figure 1-11    */
#include <stdio.h>
main()
{
/* Declarations */
     int a;
     float b,c;        /* Notice multiple declaration */
/* Assignments */
     a= 1024;
     b= a/2.0;
     c= b+a;
/* Display output */
     printf("The result = %f\n",c);
}
```

The output of this program is:

```
The result = 1536.000000
```

Here the expression "a/2.0" is assigned to the variable "b," then the sum of "a" and "b" is assigned to the variable "c." Finally, the result stored in "c" is displayed preceded by a suitable text string.

You must have noticed in Figure 1-10 that an integer value (512) was assigned to a float variable, and the result was a correct float number (512.000000); however, the opposite will lead to truncation of the fraction part, if any. The following example demonstrates this truncation when dividing 8 by 3. See Figure 1-12.

```
/*    Figure 1-12    */
#include <stdio.h>
main()
{
/* Declarations */
     int a,b;
/* Assignments */
     a= 8;
     b= a/3;
/* Display output */
     printf("%d\n",b);
}
```

The output is:

```
2
```

DRILL 1-1

The following three examples are different trials to display the value
of the fraction "3/4"; only the last one is correct. Try them all to see
the different responses of the compiler to errors. C compilers are
different in responses. Some of them may compile the program
without any error messages but result in an erroneous output.

```
/*   Figure 1-13   */
#include <stdio.h>
main()
{
    printf("%d\n",3/4);
}


/*   Figure 1-14   */
#include <stdio.h>
main()
{
    printf("%f\n",3/4);
}


/*   Figure 1-15   */
#include <stdio.h>
main()
{
    printf("%f\n",3.0/4.0);
}
```

MULTIPLE ASSIGNMENT   Multiple assignment is possible in C.
You can, for instance, assign the value 24 to more than one variable x,
y, and z using one statement as follows:

```
x = y = z = 24;
```

Another shortcut is to declare a variable and assign it a value in one
statement like:

```
int price_of_unit=99;
float radius=3.65;
```

This is called variable initialization.

The following example demonstrates these shortcuts, as well as
multiple display of all the variables using one **printf** function:

```
/*   Figure 1-16   */
#include <stdio.h>
main()
{
    int a,b,c;
    float x=3.4;
    a=b=c=24;
    printf("a=%d,\nb=%d,\nc=%d, and\nx=%f\n",a,b,c,x);
}
```

The output of the program is:

```
a=24,
b=24,
c=24, and
x=3.400000
```

TIP

It is well known that, when locating syntax errors, many C compilers always "talk about something else!" Try to remove a semicolon or a single comment character from a program, and compile it. Only rarely does the error message tell you about the missing character, but it may tell you instead about everything else in the world. With such a feature, you have to be careful when writing your statements. This is much easier than trying to figure out afterwards what the mistake was.

1-5 FORMATTED OUTPUT

The function **printf** is called "The **print** formatted output function," because it enables the programmer to *format* the output using either strings that appear in the output, or format characters such as **%d** and **%f**. You may wish to see the number 75.000000 displayed in a more manageable form like 75 or 75.00. This is done by using *modifiers* along with the format characters in order to specify the required field width.

The format **%.0f** will suppress all the zeros to the right of the decimal point, while the format **%.2f** will keep two zeros only, and so forth. Let us look at some examples in Figure 1-17.

```
/*   Figure 1-17   */
#include <stdio.h>
main()
{
    float x;
    x=75;
    printf("%.0f\n",x);
```

```
    printf("%.1f\n",x);
    printf("%.2f\n",x);
}
```

The output is:

```
75
75.0
75.00
```

The value of "x" is displayed three times in three different formats: the first one without any decimal places, the second with one decimal place, and the third with two decimal places.

What if there is a number containing fractions? The number will be rounded to the required number of decimal places, as stated in the format. The following example shows different approximations of the number "0.75":

```
/*   Figure 1-18    */
#include <stdio.h>
main()
{
    printf("%.0f\n",3.0/4.0);
    printf("%.1f\n",3.0/4.0);
    printf("%.2f\n",3.0/4.0);
}
```

The output is:

```
1
0.8
0.75
```

DRILL 1-2

Write a program to assign the number 3.45678 to a variable named "number," then display two outputs:

```
1- The "number" rounded to the nearest integer value.
2- The "number" rounded to two decimal places.
```

Display each output on a separate line, preceded by the suitable text.

1-6 THE SINGLE CHARACTER VARIABLE

The third type of variable, in addition to **int** and **float**, is the **char** variable that can only hold a single character. Any data character can be stored in a **char** variable, including unprintable characters.

Character variables are declared using the **char** keyword. For example; to declare a variable "b" of the type **char** write the statement:

```
char b;
```

To assign a character to this variable, it must be enclosed in single quotes:

```
b = 'X';
```

It is now time to introduce the conversion specifier **%c** (which stands for "character"), which is used with **char** type variables. In the following example you declare the variable "first_letter," assign it a value "A," then display its contents using the **%c** conversion specifier.

```
/*   Figure 1-19    */
#include <stdio.h>
main()
{
    char first_letter;
    first_letter='A';
    printf("%c\n",first_letter);
}
```

The output is:

```
A
```

If you use the conversion specifier **%d** to display the contents of the variable "first_letter" instead, you get the ASCII value of the character instead of the character itself (see the ASCII codes in appendix A). Now add one more line to the program as follows in Figure 1-20 :

```
/*   Figure 1-20    */
#include <stdio.h>
main()
{
    char first_letter;
    first_letter='A';
    printf("%c\n",first_letter);   /* display the character */
    printf("%d\n",first_letter);   /* display the ASCII of the character */
}
```

The output is:

```
A
65
```

This program makes clear the meaning of the name "conversion specifiers." As you can see, they are used to convert the type of the output data.

Without using any variables you can just write the statement:

```
printf("%c\n",65);
```

which gives the output "A."

You can also write the statement:

```
printf("%d\n",'A');
```

which gives the output "65."

1-7 TEXT STRINGS AND POINTERS

Strings in C are handled differently than in any other language.

When a text string is stored in the memory, you keep track of the first character by storing its address in a special type of variable called a *pointer*.

Knowing the beginning address and the length of the string, the program can locate it. This means that a pointer is a variable containing an address of another variable (rather than data). Pointers play a very important role in C, and they can point to any type of data.

DECLARING POINTERS The pointer is declared using the indirection operator (*****). For example, if a pointer "a" is pointing to an integer, it is declared as:

```
int *a;
```

If "a" is a pointer to a character, it is declared as:

```
char *a;
```

INITIALIZATION OF CHARACTER POINTERS In the following example, a *character pointer* "a" is used to point to the location of the first character in the string "Hello again." Then the value of "a" is displayed using the new conversion specifier %s (which stands for "string"), which is of course used with strings.

```
/*   Figure 1-21   */
#include <stdio.h>
main()
{
    char *a;
    a="Hello again.";
    printf("%s\n",a);
}
```

The output is:

```
Hello again.
```

In this example "a" is a *pointer to a char*, while "*a" is the *data being pointed to*, which is actually the first letter in the string (H).

The example in Figure 1-22 demonstrates handling two strings using pointers:

```
/*  Figure 1-22   */
#include <stdio.h>
main()
{
    char *a,*b;
    a="Hi, I am the string pointed to by the pointer a.";
    b="Hello, I am the string pointed to by the pointer b. ";
    printf("%s\n%s\n",a,b);
}
```

The output is:

```
Hi, I am the string pointed to by the pointer a.
Hello, I am the string pointed to by the pointer b.
```

EXAMINING MEMORY LOCATIONS In order to make sure that you understand the meaning of the pointer, examine the output of the program in Figure 1-23. This program points to the string "Hello again" with the pointer "a." Then, using the proper conversion specifier, you can examine the addresses and contents of variables. A new conversion specifier %p is introduced in the program, which is used to convert the output to hexadecimal numbers.

```
/*  Figure 1-23   */
#include <stdio.h>
main()
{
    char *a;
    a="Hello again ";
    printf("%s\n",a);
    printf("%c\n",*a);
    printf("%d\n",a);
    printf("%p\n",a);
    printf("%d\n",*a);
}
```

The output of this program is:

```
Hello again
H
168
00A8
72
```

The first **printf** statement displays the string itself by the use of the conversion specifier %s. The second one displays the character pointed to by the pointer, using the conversion specifier %c. The third and the fourth **printf** statements display the address contained in the pointer in decimal and hexadecimal respectively, using the conversion specifiers %d and %p. The last **printf** statement displays the ASCII of the first character in the string (72 is the ASCII of the letter H).

Although you are dealing with the same variable "a" or "*a," the output differs according to the conversion specifier used in the **printf** statement.

DRILL 1-3

Write a program to display the following menu, using only one **printf** statement.

```
            MAIN MENU
------------------------------------
1- WordPerfect.
2- Lotus 1-2-3.
3- dBASE IV.
4- AutoCAD.
------------------------------------
Press the required number:
```

SUMMARY

> The boldface, in the formulas, represents the keywords and syntax, while the rest is supplied by the programmer.

In this chapter you have tasted the flavor of C without going deeply into the details of the language. The following are the key points to remember:

1. The C program starts with the directives, followed by the **main** block which contains the successive statements of the program separated by semicolons. The **main** block is contained between braces.

2. The main block starts with declarations followed by the executive statements.

3. The **printf** function is used for formatted output. It is used in the form:

    ```
    printf("format", argument_1, argument_2, ...);
    ```

4. The conversion specifiers are used to convert the output to the required type. They can be modified to control the format of the output, in which case they are called format characters or format specifiers. You also learned how to use the following conversion specifiers:

%d	for decimal integers,
%f	for float numbers,
%s	for strings,
%c	for characters, and
%p	for hexadecimal numbers (addresses).

5. You know three types of data and variables:

int	for integer type,
float	for floating point type, and
char	for character type.

6. You know also how to name the variables using identifiers.

7. You can use the assignment statement and simple arithmetic expressions using arithmetic operators such as:

   +, −, *, /

8. You were introduced to the pointer variable and one of its applications to help in the handling of strings, and also the indirection operator ***** that helps in creating pointers. The next chapter contains a second round with pointers and strings.

Chapter Two

INPUT AND OUTPUT

2-1 FORMATTED INPUT

You already used the function **printf** to display formatted output. There is a similar function for data entry from the keyboard that uses formatted input. This is the **scanf** function, demonstrated in the program Figure 2-1.

```
/*   Figure 2-1   */
#include <stdio.h>
main()
{
    float x,y,z;
    scanf("%f", &x);
    scanf("%f", &y);
    z=x+y;
    printf("The sum of the two numbers:%.2f\n",z);
}
```

In this program, three variables are declared (x, y, and z). Values of "x" and "y" are to be entered from the keyboard using the **scanf** function, while the value of "z" is calculated as the sum of "x" and "y."

The **scanf** function uses the same format characters as the **printf** function to describe the type of the expected input. As you can see in the example, the format character ("%f") comes between the double quotes, while the variable "x" (or "y") comes as an argument preceded by a comma. A closer look at the **scanf** function in the program shows that the **scanf** function does not use the variables "x" and "y" themselves, but rather a new type of pointer, **&x** and **&y**. The character **&** is called the *address-of operator*, while **&x** is the address containing the variable "x" and is called the *address pointer*.

When this program runs, it waits for the user to supply the value of "x," followed by **Enter**; then it waits for the value of "y," followed by

Enter. Assuming that you entered the value of "x" as 2.25 and the value of "y" as 5, the sum is calculated and displayed in a format like:

```
The sum of the two numbers:7.25
```

The supplied input values can be separated either by pressing **Enter,** or by leaving a blank space between the numbers.

MULTIPLE VARIABLES PER STATEMENT As with **printf,** the **scanf** function can take more than one variable as in Figure 2-2.

```
/*   Figure 2-2   */
#include <stdio.h>
main()
{
    float x,y,z;
    scanf("%f%f", &x,&y);
    z=x+y;
    printf("The sum of %.2f and %.2f is: %.2f\n",x,y,z);
}
```

If you enter two values as:

>   2.25 (followed by **Enter**)
>   7.75 (followed by **Enter**)

or, as:

>   2.25 7.75 (followed by **Enter**)

The output comes in the form:

```
The sum of 2.25 and 7.75 is: 10.00
```

MIXED TYPES OF VARIABLES The **scanf** function accepts mixed types of data, provided that the proper format characters are used for each item. In the following program, use the type **int** for "x," and the type **float** for "y"; of course the sum must be of the type **float** (otherwise, it will be truncated).

```
/*   Figure 2-3   */
#include <stdio.h>
main()
{
    int x;
    float y,z;
    scanf("%d%f", &x,&y);
    z=x+y;
    printf("The sum of %d and %.2f is: %.2f\n",x,y,z);
}
```

For input like: 2 3.25 you get the output:

```
The sum of 2 and 3.25 is: 5.25
```

INPUT SEPARATORS If you like to separate your input with a comma, you must include the comma between the format characters as in Figure 2-4:

```
/*   Figure 2-4     */
#include <stdio.h>
/* Input separators */
main()
{
    int x;
    float y,z;
    scanf("%d,%f", &x,&y);   /* inputs are separated by a comma */
    z=x+y;
    printf("The sum of %d and %.2f is: %.2f\n",x,y,z);
}
```

With this program you supply the input values as:

    2,3.67

Neither does the **scanf** function use the new-line character (**\n**), nor do you need it, as long as you press **Enter**.

THE USER PROMPT One deficiency of the **scanf** function is that it cannot display strings while waiting for user input. This will require using an additional function like the **printf** in order to display a message as a prompt for the user to remind him/her of the required data item. Look at the next program where the **printf** statement precedes each **scanf** function as a reminder:

```
/*   Figure 2-5     */
#include <stdio.h>
/* Using printf() for user prompt */
main()
{
    float x,y,z;
    printf("Enter the first number:");
    scanf("%f", &x);
    printf("Enter the second number:");
    scanf("%f", &y);
    z=x+y;
    printf("The sum of the two numbers: %.2f\n",z);
}
```

The following is a sample run of the program:

```
Enter the first number:2.25
Enter the second number:3.75
The sum of the two numbers: 6.00
```

21

DRILL 2-1

Write a program to accept an ASCII number from the keyboard and display the corresponding character.

CAUTION
The **scanf** function is not recommended for entering text strings from the keyboard.

2-2 A CLOSER LOOK AT TEXT STRINGS

You stored text before using a character pointer to the first character in order to mark the beginning of the string. Actually, whenever a string is stored in memory, the **NULL** character (ASCII code zero) is added to its end; in this way the end of the string is marked and, consequently, its length can be determined. This method is more efficient than methods used in other languages, as it puts no restrictions on the length of the string.

There are 2 ways for storing text strings in **C**:

- Using character pointers
- Using character arrays

In the second method, a predefined memory space is reserved for the string.

DECLARATION OF A CHARACTER ARRAY   In order to use character arrays, you start by declaring the name and the size of the array. For example:

```
char employee_name[20];
```

This declaration reserves twenty locations in memory; the last one is reserved for the **NULL** character.

The assignment for this array is done using the function **strcpy**, which copies the string characters into the array elements. In Figure 2-6 the **strcpy** function is used to copy the string literal "Hello again" into the array "a" and then the array is displayed using **printf**. When you use the function **strcpy** in your program, you must include the header file **string.h** at the beginning.

```
/*   Figure 2-6   */
#include <stdio.h>
#include <string.h>
main()
{
    char a[20];
    strcpy(a,"Hello again");
    printf("%s\n",a);
}
```

The output is:

```
Hello again
```

When the **printf** function is executed, it reads and displays the contents of the array memory locations one after the other. Each time it checks for the **NULL** character; if it finds it, it stops.

When you declare an array like **a[20]**, the elements of the array are numbered from 0 to 19. They are referred to as:

```
a[0], a[1], a[2],...,a[19].
```

You don't have to use all the locations of the array to store the string. In the example, only the first twelve elements are occupied by data; the last of them contains the **NULL** character. You can examine each element in the array using the **printf** function and the conversion specifier **%c** or **%d**.

CAUTION

Don't do this:

```
char a[20];
a="Hello again";
```

This won't work or even compile correctly. The reason for this is that the array name (a) is considered a constant. It cannot be modified or assigned a value. The program recognizes the name "a" as the pointer storing the address of the first array element (**a[0]**); it is equivalent to **&a[0]**.

This is not the case when you declare a character pointer (***a**), where the pointer is a variable.

With character pointers you may do this:

```
char *a;
a="Hello again.";
```

or this:

```
char *a="Hello again.";
```

2-3 UNFORMATTED STRING INPUT

As I mentioned earlier, the **scanf** function is not recommended for entering strings. There are, however, many alternatives in **C** to input text strings. Actually, the most common method of data input used by programmers is to accept all data items as strings from the keyboard and then convert them to the proper type before processing.

THE FUNCTION gets   The name of the function **gets** stands for "get string." It reads a string from the keyboard, adds the **NULL** character to it, and assigns it to the required variable, which comes as an argument of the function. Look at the following example where the value of the variable employee_name is entered using the **gets** function:

```
/*   Figure 2-7     */
#include <stdio.h>
main()
{
    char employee_name[20];
    gets(employee_name);
    printf("Employee: %s\n",employee_name);
}
```

Here you can type a complete name including spaces (one thing you cannot do with **scanf**) and other characters, and when you press **Enter** the name is read and assigned to the variable employee_name.

If you try this program using a name like "Dixon, S. A.," you get the output:

```
Employee: Dixon, S. A.
```

Notice that the declared array size must be at least equal to the number of characters plus one. So if you expect an input string of length 20 characters, you would declare the array as:

```
    char employee_name[21];
```

or you may wish to declare it explicitly as:

```
    char employee_name[20+1];
```

THE FUNCTION fgets   This function reads a string from a file or a physical device, which is defined using one of the function's arguments. The function **fgets**, when used for keyboard input, takes the form:

```
    fgets(a, n, stdin);
```

where:

a is the string character array,

n is the maximum number of input characters, and

stdin is the standard input device (the keyboard).

When the **Enter** key is pressed to terminate the data entry, the new-line character (\n) and the **NULL** character are added to the string. So, with this function, you must allow for two extra characters in the declared array size. In the following example, the function **fgets** is used to read the "employee_name" up to 20 characters.

```
/*   Figure 2-8    */
#include <stdio.h>
main()
{
    char employee_name[20+2];
    fgets(employee_name,22,stdin);
    printf("Employee: %s\n",employee_name);
}
```

DRILL 2-2

Write a program to input from the keyboard the "item_name," which is a text string of length up to 40 characters, and the "item_price," which is a float number. Print the contents of the two variables in the proper format.

2-4 UNFORMATTED STRING OUTPUT

As with unformatted input, there are some functions that send the output directly to the screen or other output devices, without any conversion or format.

THE FUNCTION puts This is the conjugate of the **gets** function. Its name stands for "put string." It uses one argument, which can be either a data item (a string literal) or a variable, and puts it on the screen. The following example in Figure 2-9 prompts the user to enter the employee name using the **puts** function, then accepts the user input using the **gets** function. Finally, it displays what has been entered (the employee name).

```
/*   Figure 2-9    */
#include <stdio.h>
main()
{
    char employee_name[20+1];
    puts("Enter employee name: ");
    gets(employee_name);
    puts(employee_name);
}
```

With the function **puts,** the new-line character is automatically written as the last character in the string.

THE FUNCTION fputs This function is the contrast of **fgets.** It outputs the data using two arguments: the data string or variable, and the name of the output device. The function **fputs,** when used with the screen, takes the form:

   fputs(a, stdout);

where:

   a   is the string character array, and
   stdout   is the standard output device (the screen).

If you replace the name of the device **stdout** by the name **stdprn** (the printer), the output is sent to the printer.

The following example in Figure 2-10 displays the string "Hello" to the screen. Pay attention to the third line in the main block, which contains the new-line character (\n). If you want to display the string on a new line, you must use this statement because unlike the function **puts,** the function **fputs** doesn't write the new-line character automatically. Try to comment this line by enclosing it between the two comment characters and inspect the output for two or more runs. Every "Hello" in this case will be catenated to the others as one string.

Notice that you can add the new-line character to the string itself (as in "\nHello"), even though this example does not do it this way.

```
/*   Figure 2-10    */
#include <stdio.h>
#include <string.h>
main()
{
    char buf[80];
    strcpy(buf,"Hello");
    fputs("\n",stdout);     /* Try the program without this line */
    fputs(buf,stdout);
}
```

The following example demonstrates using the two functions **fgets** and **fputs** together. It displays the question "How are you today?" using **fputs,** and when you enter the answer, your response is stored in the variable "resp." Both the prompt and the response are sent to the printer, and they appear in one line.

```
/*   Figure 2-11    */
#include <stdio.h>
main()
{
    char resp[80];
    fputs("How are you today? ",stdout);
    fgets(resp,80,stdin);
    fputs("How are you today? ",stdprn);
    fputs(resp,stdprn);
}
```

The printed output looks like:

```
How are you today? Just fine, thank you.
```

2-5 CHARACTER INPUT

There are some functions in **C** that handle characters only. These functions are useful in some applications when the user is prompted to choose an item or a number from a menu and press one key only, such as the number of the choice or the first letter of the choice name.

Three input functions are available in most compilers: the original **getchar** function which was introduced by Kernighan and Ritchie, and the new functions **getch** and **getche** which were added later to suit the microcomputer interactive environment. The name **getchar** stands for "get character." The three functions are used without arguments, but you must keep the empty parentheses.

THE FUNCTION getchar   This function reads one character from the keyboard after the new-line character is received (when you press **Enter**).

The following program demonstrates the use of the function **getchar**. It begins with declaring an integer variable "ascii," then the function itself is assigned to this variable. This means that the character received by the function will be contained in the variable "ascii." The first **printf** function displays the contents of the variable "ascii" in the character format (**%c**) preceded by the string "The character." The second **printf** function displays the same variable in the decimal format (**%d**) preceded by the string "corresponds to the ASCII."

```
/*   Figure 2-12    */
#include <stdio.h>
main()
{
    int ascii;
    printf("\nType a character and press ENTER: ");
    ascii=getchar();
    printf("The character %c ",ascii);
    printf("corresponds to the ASCII %d ",ascii);
}
```

A sample run of this program gives the output:

```
Type a character and press ENTER: B         ----> Your input
The character B corresponds to the ASCII 66    ----> The program output
```

The function **getchar** can also be assigned to a variable of the type **char**. Just replace the word **int** by the word **char**, as in Figure 2-13, and the program still gives the same results.

```
/*   Figure 2-13    */
#include <stdio.h>
main()
{
    char ascii;
    printf("\nType a character and press ENTER: ");
    ascii=getchar();
    printf("The character %c ",ascii);
    printf("corresponds to the ASCII %d ",ascii);
}
```

Notice that if you enter more than one character, the function **getchar** still reads the first one only. Also, if you press **Enter** only, you get the number "10," which is the ASCII code for the new-line character (see the ASCII codes in appendix A).

THE FUNCTIONS getch AND getche   These two functions are very similar, as they respond without pressing the **Enter** key. The difference is that with the function **getche** the echo of the pressed key is displayed on the screen (the letter "e" stands for "echo"), but with the function **getch** there is no echoing. This example demonstrates the difference:

```
/*   Figure 2-14    */
#include <stdio.h>
#include <conio.h>
main()
{
    int option;
/* The character is displayed when pressed */
    printf("\nMake a choice and press a number:");
    option=getche();
```

```
/* The character is not displayed when pressed */
    printf("\nMake a choice and press a number:");
    option=getch();
}
```

When you use the function **getch** or **getche** in a program, you must include the header file **conio.h**.

DRILL 2-3

Add one more step to the menu created in Drill 1-3. After you display the menu lines and the prompt message, accept a character from the user and display it, as shown in the following figure:

```
/*   Figure 2-15   */
            MAIN MENU
-------------------------------------
1- WordPerfect.
2- Lotus 1-2-3.
3- dBASE IV.
4- AutoCAD.
-------------------------------------
Press the required number:          ----> The user input

Your choice is: 2                   ----> The program output
```

This is the second step in creating a user menu.

2-6 CHARACTER OUTPUT

Instead of using the function **printf** to display only one character, it is better to use a simple unformatted function that writes the character to the screen. C contains many functions that handle characters, especially with file processing.

THE FUNCTION putchar The function **putchar** (stands for "put character") uses one argument, which can be a character variable or the character itself contained in single quotes. Look at the following example:

```
/*   Figure 2-16   */
#include <stdio.h>
main()
{
    char x='A';
    putchar(x);
    putchar('B');
}
```

The output is:

AB

Here the character "A" is displayed as the contents of the variable "x" using the function **putchar**. Then the character "B" is displayed directly without using variables.

The **putchar** function does not display the new-line character. Unlike the **printf** function it does not use any control or format characters, and the only way to leave a blank line after the displayed character is to use another **putchar**.

The following example demonstrates using the function including displaying the new-line character (**\n**). A comparison is made between **printf** and **putchar** in the same program.

```
/*    Figure 2-17    */
#include <stdio.h>
main()
{
    char x='A';
    putchar(x);
    putchar('\n');        /* blank line */
    printf("%c\n",x);
}
```

The output is:

A
A

THE FUNCTION putc   This function is intended for files, but the output can be redirected to any standard device like the screen (**stdout**) or the printer (**stdprn**). It takes the form:

```
putc(a, device);
```

where:

    a   is the character to be sent to the output, and
    device is the output device.

In the following example the device name **stdout** is used to have the output displayed on the screen. You may wish to try it with the printer by changing the device name to **stdprn**.

```
/*    Figure 2-18    */
#include <stdio.h>
main()
{
    char x='A';
    putc(x,stdout);
    putc('\n',stdout);
}
```

SUMMARY

> The boldface, in the formulas, represents the keywords and syntax, while the rest is supplied by the programmer.

1. In this chapter you were introduced to the most important I/O (input output) functions of **C**. The following is a summary of the functions used so far.

   - Formatted output function (discussed in Chapter Two):

     printf("format", argument_1, argument_2, ...**)**;

   - Formatted input function:

     scanf("format", pointer_1, pointer_2, ...**)**;

   - String input functions:

     gets(string**)**;
     fgets(string, length, device**)**;

   - String output functions:

     puts(string**)**;
     fputs(string, device**)**;

   - Character input functions:

     getchar();
     getch();
     getche();

   - Character output functions:

     putchar(character**)**;
     putc(character, device**)**;

In the output functions above, the word "string" stands for a string literal or a string variable (a pointer to a character array), while in the input functions it stands for a string variable. The word "character" in the output functions stands for either a character or a character variable, while in the input functions it stands for a character variable.

Also the "device" means either a standard device name or a file (files explained later).

2. In addition to I/O functions, you used the function **strcpy** to copy the contents of a string literal into a string variable.

3. You also know two different ways to declare a string variable:

   - The character pointer:
     ```
     char *variable;
     ```

   - The character array:
     ```
     char variable[size];
     ```

Keep in mind that in both cases the string is stored in an "array," the first character of which is pointed to by the string variable (the pointer). The second method is safer, however, as it allocates memory locations in advance according to the declared size of the array.

4. Finally, you know the syntax to declare a character variable:
   ```
   char variable;
   ```

The character constant must be included in single quotes whether it is a printable character such as 'A' or a control character such as '\n'.

Chapter Three

PUTTING THINGS TOGETHER

3-1 LITERALS

The data values usually are called constants. In **C**, however, some authors refer to them as *literals* or *literal constants*. In any case, the literals can be one of the following types:

- Integers
- Real (floating point)
- Characters
- Character strings

The integer numbers can belong to the decimal, the hexadecimal, or octal numbering systems. The following rules are used to indicate the numbering system:

- The prefix **0x** or **0X** is used for hexadecimal numbers.
- The prefix **0** is used for octal numbers.
- No prefix is used for decimal numbers.

For example, the number 11 is expressed in the three systems as follows:

```
.decimal        11
.hexadecimal    0xB or 0XB
.octal          013
```

The real numbers can be expressed in two ways, in the decimal form or in scientific (exponential) notation. The number expressed in scientific notation is divided into two parts separated by the letter **E** or **e**. The first part is the mantissa, while the second part is the exponent, which represents a power of ten. The following are some examples using scientific notation:

1.234E+2 or 1.234e+2 is equal to 123.4
1.234E–2 or 1.234e–2 is equal to .01234

Scientific notation is useful to express very large and very small numbers.

The character literals, as mentioned before, must be enclosed between single quotes like 'A', and the string literals must be enclosed between double quotes like "Hello World."

DRILL 3-1

Which of the following are valid numeric literals?

    a. 4F
    b. 0x4F
    c. 017
    d. 018

3-2 BASIC DATA TYPES

The memory locations which store data values are called variables. The variables are identified by names (identifiers) and are classified in various types. The variable types (or data types) must be declared at the beginning of the program.

You already used different data types (such as **int, float**, and **char**) in declarations of your variables in the previous chapters, but there are a few more types. In all, the **C** language contains five basic types of data which correspond to different storage sizes and ranges of data values. They are shown in Table 3-1.

Table 3-1   Basic C Data Types

Data type	Size in bits	Range
char	8	−128 to 127
int	18	−32,768 to 32767
float	32	3.4E−38 to 3.4E+38 (accuracy up to 7 digits)
double	64	1.7E−308 to 1.7E+308 (accuracy up to 15 digits)
void	0	without value

For each type there is a limited *range* for the numbers which can be stored. For example, the **int** type can hold numbers in the range from −32,768 to 32,767. The two limits of the positive and negative numbers are not equal because the computer treats the zero as a positive number. The **double** type is used to hold real numbers (floating point), but of a higher storage range and *accuracy* than the type **float**. The **void** type, which is unique to **C**, is used to create generic pointers and declare void functions, as discussed later.

TIP

The compiler does not check or warn you if you stored a value that does not fit into the variable type. You must be cautious of the limits.

3-3 TYPE CONVERSION

When you mix different types together in one expression, the compiler automatically carries out the proper conversion of types. For example, when adding a **float** to an integer, the result will be of the **float** type. In fact, when the compiler meets different types it raises all of them to the same type (temporarily) before evaluating the expression. So if one expression contains **char**, **int**, **float**, and **double**, then all the types are converted to double before any manipulation of the operands. Needless to say, the declared types are not changed for good, and they regain the original type (the declared type) right after the operation.

The most important thing is that you must be aware of the conversion rules in order to use the proper format character when you display the results using the **printf** function.

The following example adds two values, one stored in an integer variable "a," the second is stored in a **float** variable "b," and the result is stored in a variable "c" of the **float** type.

```
/*   Figure 3-1   */
#include <stdio.h>
/*   type conversion   */
main()
{
    int a=300;
    float b=50.25;
    float c;
    c=a+b;
    printf("\n%f",c);
}
```

The output of this program is as expected:

```
350.250000
```

Now look at this example, where you decide to get your output as an integer type by declaring "c" as an **int**. The fraction will be truncated from the output as shown in the following program.

```
/*   Figure 3-2   */
#include <stdio.h>
/*   type conversion   */
/*   truncation   */
main()
{
    int a=300;
    float b=50.25;
    int c;
    c=a+b;
    printf("\n%d",c);
}
```

The output is:

```
350
```

You could get lucky if you don't have a fraction part. In that case you would get a correct result, but don't try it.

THE RANGE PROBLEM The fraction part, however, is not the only problem. If you keep in mind that the type **int** is stored in two bytes, while the type **float** is stored in four, then you should expect that the size of the number may not fit in the new store. Look at the following example where the result cannot fit into two bytes. The output is nonsense.

```
/*   Figure 3-3   */
#include <stdio.h>
/*   type conversion   */
/*   erroneous results   */
main()
```

```
{
    int a=32767;
    float b=50;
    int c;
    c=a+b;
    printf("\n%d",c);
}
```

The output is:

```
-32719
```

THE TYPE CASTS Consider the case if you want to divide two integers "a/b," where the result must be an integer. You may want to force the output to be a **float** in order to keep the fraction part of the division. The cast operator is used in this case. It will do the conversion without any loss of data.

The form of the cast is:

```
(type) expression
```

Look at the following example where the cast **(float)** is used to force the type of the division result to be **float**.

```
/*   Figure 3-4    */
#include <stdio.h>
/*   type conversion - using the cast    */
main()
{
    int a, b;
    a=3;
    b=2;
    printf("\n%f",(float)a/b);
}
```

The output is:

```
1.500000
```

DRILL 3-2

Evaluate the following expressions:

   a. given:
```
float x=5.5;  float y=4;.
```

   evaluate:
```
(int) x + (int) y
```

   b. given:
```
int x=9;  int y=4;
```

evaluate:

```
x / y
(float) x / y
(float) x / (float) y
```

3-4 THE PRECISION OF RESULTS

The range problem is different from the precision problem. As mentioned before, the **double** type is twice as precise as the **float** type. In order to understand the limited precision of the **float** type, try to use a large number of more than seven digits. In the next example the variable "a" holds the number 123456789.0, which is beyond the accuracy of the float type. If you examine the output, you realize that after the seventh digit the number has been rounded, resulting in corruption of data.

```
/*   Figure 3-5   */
#include <stdio.h>
/* float numbers accuracy */
main()
{
    float a;
    a=123456789.0;
    printf("The value of a=%f",a);
}
```

The output is:

```
The value of a=123456792.000000
```

To overcome this problem use the **double** type which is capable of holding such large numbers with up to 15 digits of accuracy. Here is the same example with the proper type used.

```
/*   Figure 3-6   */
#include <stdio.h>
/* double numbers accuracy */
main()
{
    double a;
    a=123456789.0;
    printf("The value of a=%f",a);
}
```

The output is:

```
The value of a=123456789.000000
```

3-5 DATA TYPE MODIFIERS

The basic data types may be modified by adding special keywords called *data type modifiers* to produce new features or new types. The modifiers are:

signed
unsigned
long
short

Except with **void** type, the modifiers can be used with all basic data types according to the combinations shown in Table 3-2.

Table 3-2   C Basic Types and Modifiers

Data Type	Size in bits	Range
char	8	−128 to 127
unsigned char	8	0 to 255
signed char	8	−128 to 127
int	16	−32,768 to 32,767
short	16	−32,768 to 32,767
short int	16	−32,768 to 32,767
unsigned	16	0 to 65,535
unsigned int	16	0 to 65,535
unsigned short	16	0 to 65,535
signed	16	−32,768 to 32,767
signed int	16	−32,768 to 32,767
long	32	−2,147,483,648 to 2,147,483,647
long int	32	−2,147,483,648 to 2,147,483,647
unsigned long	32	0 to 4,294,967,295
signed long	32	−2,147,483,648 to 2,147,483,647
float	32	3.4E−38 to 3.4E+38
double	64	1.7E−308 to 1.7E+308
long double	80	3.4E−4932 to 1.1E+4932 (19 digits of precision)

Note that if you don't specify the basic type, it is by default **int**. For example, **short** is the same as **short int**. Also the **signed** modifier is the default, which means that the type **signed int** is the same as **int**. This way some types in the table are just duplicates of others.

As you see in the table, using the **unsigned** modifier means doubling the maximum range of the stored number. The **unsigned** data types, however, hold positive numbers only (including zero). In other words, it is a trade-off between using negative numbers and doubling the storage range.

3-6 OUTPUT FORMAT

When printing the value stored in a variable, as mentioned in Chapter One, you must use the suitable conversion specifier/format commands with the **printf** function. All of the output conversion specifiers and their meanings are shown in Table 3-3.

Table 3-3   The printf Conversion Specifiers

Conversion Specifier	Meaning of the output format
%c	Character
%s	String of characters
%d	Decimal integer
%i	Decimal integer
%f	Floating point
%e or %E	Scientific notation
%g or %G	Scientific notation or floating point, whichever is shorter
%u	Unsigned decimal integer
%o	Octal number
%x or %X	Hexadecimal number
%p	Pointer
%n	The associated argument is an integer pointer, into which is placed the number of characters printed so far.
%%	Displays the % sign

You already used some of these specifiers, actually the most important of them, with the **printf** function. The following is an example to demonstrate the use of the conversion specifiers **%x** and **%o** to convert an **int** to a hexadecimal number and an octal number. Note that you cannot convert a real number to either hexadecimal or octal.

```
/*   Figure 3-7    */
#include <stdio.h>
main()
{
    int a;
    a=65;
    printf("\nThe value of a= %d",a);
    printf("\nThe value of a in hexadecimal= %x",a);
    printf("\nThe value of a in octal= %o",a);
}
```

The output is:

```
The value of a= 65
The value of a in hexadecimal= 41
The value of a in octal= 101
```

The next example demonstrates the use of scientific notation to display the number "−100."

```
/*    Figure 3-8    */
#include <stdio.h>
main()
{
    float x;
    x=-100.0;
    printf("\nThe value of x= %f",x);
    printf("\nThe value of x= %e",x);
}
```

The output is:

```
The value of x= -100.000000
The value of x= -1.000000e+02
```

FORMAT MODIFIERS You know as well that the format commands can be modified to produce a formatted output such as **%.2f** and **%.0f**.

In general, the modifier describes the output field in the form:

W.d

where:

W	is the field width, and
d	is the number of decimal places.

Modifiers can also modify decimal integers and text strings to describe the width of the output field, like **%4d** or **%6s**. In this case the numbers or the strings are right justified. You can also insert leading zeros by adding a zero before the width of the field, as in **%04d** or **%06.2f**.

The following are some examples of using modifiers with different data types:

	Format	*Output*
1.	**printf("%.2f",12.3456)**	12.35
2.	**printf("%10.2f",1234.567)**	1234.57
3.	**printf("%d",12)**	12
4.	**printf("%4d",12)**	12
5.	**printf("%04d",12)**	0012

41

6. **printf("%s","12345")**   12345
7. **printf("%10s","12345")**   12345

In the first example the number is rounded to two decimal places as a result of the format **.2f**. In the second example the number is printed in a ten-character field width with two decimal places according to the format **10.2f** and hence is right shifted. In the third example the integer 12 is printed in the usual way, while in the fourth it is printed in a field four characters wide in accordance with the format **4d**, and so is shifted two places to the right. In the fifth example the leading zeros appear in the field due to the format **04d**. In the sixth example the number is treated as a string, and in the last example the same string is printed in a ten-character field width.

You have to modify the format specifiers according to the data type used. For example, using the **long** modifier in the declared type implies using the modifier **l** or **L** in the format command according to the following rules:

- Long integer   **%ld**
- Double   **%lf**
- Long double   **%Lf**

In the following example, a **long double** is declared and assigned a value, then three **printf** statements are used to try to get the data stored in the variable. As you can see, only the last one succeeds, as the proper modifier **Lf** is used. In the first two statements you get meaningless values.

```
/*   Figure 3-9    */
#include <stdio.h>
main()
{
    long double x=123456789.22;
    printf("\nThe value of x= %f",x);
    printf("\nThe value of x= %lf",x);
    printf("\nThe value of x= %Lf",x);
}
```

The output is:

```
The value of x= -5.2674017371575017500000000000000000000000e+209
The value of x= -5.2674017371575017500000000000000000000000e+209
The value of x= 123456789.220000
```

DRILL 3-3

Given:

```
int a=555;
float b=555.55;
```

Evaluate the output of the statements:

```
printf("%06d",a);
printf("%e",b);
```

THE BACKSLASH CODES   You are already familiar with the new-line character (**\n**) used with the **printf** function. Actually, there are many control characters which are similar to the new-line character in that they are preceded by the backslash and may be referred to as *Escape* characters or backslash codes. The codes and their effects are summarized in Table 3-4.

Table 3-4   The Backslash Codes

Backslash code	Effect
\a	Ring the bell
\b	Backspace (BS)
\n	New line or Line Feed (LF)
\r	Carriage Return (CR)
\t	Horizontal Tab (HT)
\v	Vertical Tab (VT)
\\	Print the backslash
\'	Print a single quote
\"	Print a double quote
\xhhh	Print the character hhh, where hhh is a hexadecimal number
\ooo	Print the character ooo, where ooo is an octal number
\0	The **NULL** character

You can use the backslash codes to send almost any code to the output device, but they are more useful with unprintable characters such as the tab and the carriage return.

The following example demonstrates the use of some backslash codes. In the first line the tab code (**\t**) is used to display the string "Hello backslash codes."

In the second line the character "A" is displayed in three different ways, the first time using a tab followed by the character "A." The second time, it is displayed using another tab and the hexadecimal

ASCII code (41) for the character "A." The last one is displayed using a tab and the octal ASCII code (101).

The third line shows how to display a string inside quotes.

It is possible to use as many codes as you wish in the format part of the **printf** function.

```
/*   Figure 3-10    */
#include <stdio.h>
main()
{
/* Backslash codes */
    printf("\n\tHello\tbackslash\tcodes");
    printf("\n\t\A\t\x41\t\t\101");
    printf("\n\t\"This is how to show quotes\"");
}
```

The output is:

```
Hello    backslash        codes
A        A                A
"This is how to show quotes"
```

3-7 INPUT FORMAT

With the formatted input function **scanf** you must use the proper format specifiers in order to tell the compiler about the expected data types to be read. You have already used some of these specifiers in the preceding chapters. Here they are summarized in Table 3-5.

Table 3-5   The scanf Conversion Specifiers

Conversion Specifier	Meaning of the format to be read
%c	Character
%s	String of characters
%d	Decimal integer
%i	Decimal integer
%f	Floating point number
%e	Floating point number
%o	Octal number
%x	Hexadecimal number
%p	pointer
%n	The received integer value is equal to the number of characters read so far.

3-8 CONSTANTS

C allows you to declare variables of fixed values called *constants*. You may need to use this type of variable to declare a constant value like "pi" which maintains the same value (3.14159) all the time.

Constants are declared in the program in one of the following ways:

1. Using the **const** keyword. For example,

   ```
   const float pi=3.14159;
   ```

2. Using the **#define** directive. For example,

   ```
   #define pi  3.14159
   ```

In the first method you declare the type of the constant, while in the second method you don't. The directive **#define** must come before the program main block.

The following example demonstrates the use of the first method to declare a **const** "pi." The rest of the program calculates the perimeter of a circle from a given radius.

```
/*   Figure 3-11   */
#include <stdio.h>
main()
{
     const float pi=3.14159;
     float radius;
     printf("\nEnter radius in mm:");
     scanf("%f",&radius);
     printf("\nThe perimeter is %.2f",2*pi*radius);
}
```

If you respond to the prompt by entering a value of 25 for the radius, the output will be:

```
Enter radius in mm:25
The perimeter is 157.08
```

The second example expresses the same logic but uses the directive **#define**:

```
/*   Figure 3-12   */
#include <stdio.h>
#define pi 3.14159
main()
{
     float radius;
     printf("\nEnter radius in mm:");
     scanf("%f",&radius);
     printf("\nThe perimeter is %.2f",2*pi*radius);
}
```

45

A sample run of the program gives:

```
Enter radius in mm:25
The perimeter is 157.08
```

The reason for calling the data values "literals" rather than "constants" is to avoid confusion with the **const** variables. Actually, some languages call the **const** variables "parameters." But anyway, this is not the only confusion in **C**. You must have noticed that the symbol ***** is used as the multiplication operator and the indirection pointer operator. Also the operator **&** is used so far as the address-of pointer operator, but soon it will be used as the bitwise AND operator.

You have to be careful.

SUMMARY

1. In this chapter you have learned more about literal constants and how to express numeric constants from other numbering systems.

2. You learned also the five basic types of data: **int, float, char, double,** and **void.**

3. You know how the compiler carries out the type conversion when the expression is evaluated, and how to force the type of the result to be a certain type using the cast.

4. You are now aware of the range problem that may occur if the proper type is not used.

5. You are familiar with the type modifiers that can change the basic type characteristics, such as **signed, unsigned, long,** and **short.**

6. You have learned as well the conversion specifiers used with the **printf** function, and how to modify them to format the output.

7. You used the backslash codes to send printable or control characters to the output.

8. You know the format specifiers used with the function **scanf.**

9. Finally, you know two methods to declare and use the **const** variables whose values remain constant during the execution of the program.

DAY TWO

Chapter Four

ALL ABOUT C OPERATORS

4-1 EXPRESSIONS AND OPERATORS

Expressions can be built up from literals, variables, and operators. The operators define how the variables and literals in the expression will be manipulated. If you are coming from another computer language background, you may be familiar with three types of operators: arithmetic, relational, and logical. C, however, is very rich in operators and is sometimes called "the language of operators." C operators may be classified as:

- Arithmetic operators
- Relational operators
- Logical operators
- Assignment operators
- Pointer operators
- Special operators
- Bitwise operators

4-2 ARITHMETIC OPERATORS

Table 4-1 lists the C arithmetic operators. You dealt before with the first four operators in the table (–, +, *, /), which are used for subtraction, addition, multiplication, and division.

In this chapter you learn about three new operators: the modulo division, the increment, and the decrement operators.

Table 4-1 Arithmetic Operators

Operator	Action
−	Subtraction and unary minus
+	Addition
*	Multiplication
/	Division
%	Modulo division
− −	Decrement
++	Increment

MODULO DIVISION OPERATOR The modulo division operator (%) gives the remainder of the integer division. The following example demonstrates the use of both the division and the modulo division operators in dividing 10 by 3.

```
/*   Figure 4-1   */
#include <stdio.h>
main( )
{
    int x=10, y=3;
    printf("\nInteger division 10/3= %d",x/y);
    printf("\nRemainder of integer division 10%%3= %d",x%y);
}
```

The output is:

```
Integer division 10/3= 3
Remainder of integer division 10%3= 1
```

Notice the method used to display the operator % in the output. You may need to refer back to Table 3-3 in Chapter Three.

INCREMENT AND DECREMENT OPERATORS The increment and decrement operators are very useful operators and are not found in other languages. The operator **++** means "add 1," and the operator **− −** means "subtract 1." For example, instead of using the following expression to increment a counter:

```
a=a+1;
```

you may use the **C** expression :

```
++a;
```

Also the expression:

```
a=a-1;
```

is the same as the expression:

```
--a;
```

The two operators **++** and **− −** are useful with shortcuts. For example, instead of writing the following two statements:

```
b=b+1;
sum=a+b;
```

you can write the same logic in one step as:

```
sum=a+(++b);
```

The increment and decrement operators may precede or follow the operand, which means that the following expressions are equivalent:

```
x++;
++x;
```

In some cases, however, there is a difference. Consider the two statements:

```
sum1=a+(++b);
sum2=a+(b++);
```

In the first statement the variable "b" is incremented and then added to "a;" while in the second statement the addition takes place before the incrementing. The following program puts these two statements into action.

```
/*    Figure 4-2    */
#include <stdio.h>
main()
{
     int a=8, b=2, x=8, y=2, sum1, sum2;
/* Increment then add */
     sum1=a+(++b);
/* Add then increment */
     sum2=x+(y++);
     printf("\nSUM1=%d",sum1);
     printf("\nSUM2=%d",sum2);
}
```

The output is:

```
SUM1=11
SUM2=10
```

Notice that two typical pairs of variables are used in the program (a,b and x,y) in order to avoid mixing the values of "sum1" and "sum2."

DRILL 4-1

Initialize the variable "a" to a value 15; then examine the resulting values of the variables "a," "b," and "c" after these two operations:

```
b=a++;     and     c=++a;
```

PRECEDENCE OF ARITHMETIC OPERATORS Table 4-2 shows the precedence of arithmetic operators and their *associativity*. Associativity is the direction in which the compiler evaluates the expression. If in the same expression you have two operators of the same precedence, they are evaluated from left to right, except for increment and decrement operators, which are evaluated from right to left.

Table 4-2 Precedence of Arithmetic Operators

Operator	Associativity	Precedence
++ --	Right to left	Highest
-	Left to right	
* / %	Left to right	
+ -	Left to right	Lowest

You can always use parentheses to change the order of evaluation. For example:

```
2+8/2
(2+8)/2
```

The expression "2+8/2" is evaluated as 6 since the division is done first; while the expression "(2+8)/2" is evaluated as 5 because the addition, between the parentheses, is done first.

NOTE

The statement:

```
sum=a+ ++b;
```

is the same as the statement:

```
sum=a+(++b);
```

but the following statement is different from both:

```
sum=a+++b;
```

So, it would be a good idea to use parentheses to avoid this confusion.

4-3 RELATIONAL AND LOGICAL OPERATORS

The relational operators are used to compare values forming relational expressions. The logical operators are used to connect relational expressions together using the rules of formal logic. Both types of expressions produce *TRUE* or *FALSE* results. In **C**, FALSE is the zero, while any nonzero number is TRUE. However, the logical and relational expressions produce the value "1" for TRUE and the value "0" for FALSE.

Table 4-3 shows relational and logical operators used in **C**. They are lower in precedence than arithmetic operators. That means that the expression:

```
100 > 90+9
```

is equivalent to the expression:

```
100 > (90+9)
```

This is because in both cases the addition is evaluated first. However, you will probably feel better if you use parentheses.

Table 4-3   Relational and Logical Operators

Operator	Action
Relational Operators:	
>	Greater than
>=	Greater than or equal
<	Less than
<=	Less than or equal
==	Equal
!=	Not equal
Logical Operators:	
&&	AND
||	OR
!	NOT

NOTE

Notice that the equality operator (==) is different in **C** than in any other language. Don't confuse it with the assignment operator (=).

EVALUATION OF LOGICAL EXPRESSIONS To understand how a logical expression is evaluated consider the expression:

```
x==y && w>=z
```

This expression says: "x is equal to y AND w is greater than or equal to z." In other words the expression is evaluated as TRUE if both of the following conditions are met:

1. The expression **x==y** is evaluated as TRUE, and

2. The expression **w>=z** is evaluated as TRUE.

If you replace the AND (**&&**) by an OR (**||**), then the expression is evaluated as TRUE if either one of the two expressions (1 or 2) is evaluated as TRUE.

PRECEDENCE OF RELATIONAL AND LOGICAL OPERATORS

Table 4-4 shows the relative precedence of the relational and logical operators.

Table 4-4   Precedence of Relational and Logical Operators

Operator	Associativity	Precedence
!	Right to left	Highest
> >= < <=	Left to right	
== !=	Left to right	
&&	Left to right	
||	Left to right	Lowest

In order to see how the precedence works, look at this expression:

```
a==b && x==y || m==n
```

This expression is evaluated as TRUE if one of the following conditions is met:

1. If **a==b** is evaluated as TRUE, and **x==y** is evaluated as TRUE, or

2. If **m==n** is evaluated as TRUE.

That means that the operator **&&** is evaluated before the operator **||** because of having higher precedence. In other words, this expression is evaluated as if it had parentheses as follows:

```
(a==b && x==y) || (m==n)
```

More application for these operators later.

4-4 ASSIGNMENT OPERATORS

The assignment operator, as you know, is the simple equal sign (=). The assignment statement follows the format:

```
variable-name = expression;
```

The expression can be a single variable or literal, or it may contain variables, literals, and operators.

In **C**, as usual, shortcuts are possible. For example, instead of the statement:

```
a=a+b;
```

you may use the shorthand form:

```
a+=b;
```

Actually, the combination "+=" includes both incrementing the variable "a" by one and the assignment. It is called the *combined operator*. Many similar assignments can be made, such as:

x−=y;	is the same as	x=x−y;
x*=y;	is the same as	x=x*y;
x/=y;	is the same as	x=x/y;
x%=y;	is the same as	x=x%y;

4-5 POINTER OPERATORS

You met the pointers in the preceding chapters, and you already know the address-of operator (**&**) and the indirection operator (*****). The **&** operator returns the address of the variable. For example, if you declare an integer variable by the statement:

```
int salary;
```

then the pointer "&salary" returns the address of the variable "salary." Also, if you declare an integer pointer with the statement:

```
int *pntr;
```

then you may assign the address "&salary" to the pointer using the statement:

```
pntr=&salary;
```

In this case the pointer "pntr" points to the address of "salary." Using the operator ***** you can reach the contents of the variable "salary." Actually, the value "***pntr**" is the contents of "salary." Run the following program to examine these properties of pointers:

```
/*   Figure 4-3   */
#include <stdio.h>
main()
{
    int salary, *pntr;
    salary=3000;
    pntr=&salary;
```

```
        printf("\nThe value of salary is %d",salary);
        printf("\nThe value pointed to is %d",*pntr);
        *pntr=3333;
        printf("\nThe value of salary is %d",salary);
}
```

The output is:

```
The value of salary is 3000
The value pointed to is 3000
The value of salary is 3333
```

In this program the value of the variable "salary" is changed to "3333" by modifying the contents "*pntr."

In case of pointers to characters, as mentioned earlier, the * operator returns the value of the first character of the string being pointed to.

DRILL 4-2

Examine the address holding the variable "salary" using the proper **printf** statements to display the pointers "&salary" and "pntr." They should be the same.

4-6 SPECIAL OPERATORS

C contains different types of operators which may be classified as special or miscellaneous operators as they don't belong to any specific category. Of these special operators, the only one you have seen is the cast operator. Now you will be introduced to the **?** operator, the *comma* operator, and the sizeof operator.

THE ? OPERATOR This operator helps in building a simple conditional expression in the form:

```
variable = expression_1 ? expression_2 : expression_3;
```

This form emulates the well-known **if** statement (in most computer languages including **C**):

```
IF expression_1 THEN
    variable = expression_2
        ELSE variable = expression_3
```

In both formulas expression_1 is a relational or a logical expression. If expression_1 is evaluated as TRUE, then the variable is assigned the value of expression_2; otherwise, it is assigned the value of expression_3.

In the following example, the value of a variable "b" is determined according to whether or not the value of the variable "a" is greater than 25.

```
/*    Figure 4-4    */
#include <stdio.h>
main()
{
    int a,b;
    printf("\nEnter the value of the variable \"a\": ");
    scanf("%d",&a);
    b= a>25 ? 100 : 99;
    printf("\nThe value of the variable \"b\" is %d",b);
}
```

If you entered a value like 6 for the variable "a," then you get the following on your screen:

```
Enter the value of the variable "a": 6
The value of the variable "b" is 99
```

The conditional expression may be used inside another statement (another shortcut of **C**). In the following example you have two messages, "msg1" and "msg2." The conditional expression is embedded in the **printf** function where one of the messages is to be displayed according to the value of the variable "a." Another **printf** statement is used to display the value of the variable "b" based on the value of "a."

```
/*    Figure 4-5    */
#include <stdio.h>
main()
{
    int a, b;
    char *msg1, *msg2, *msg3;
    msg1="The value of \"a\" is greater than 25";
    msg2="The value of \"a\" is less than or equal to 25";
    msg3="The value of \"b\" is: " ;
    printf("\nEnter the value of the variable \"a\": ");
    scanf("%d",&a);
    printf("\n%s",a>25 ? msg1 : msg2);
    printf("\n%s %d",msg3,b=a>25 ? 100 :99);
}
```

A sample run of this program gives the following:

```
Enter the value of the variable "a": 77
The value of "a" is greater than 25
The value of "b" is:  100
```

THE COMMA OPERATOR   You can use the comma (,) to build a compound expression by putting several expressions inside a set of parentheses. The expressions are evaluated from left to right and the final value is the last one evaluated. Look at this expression:

```
(x=c, c=getchar())
```

Here you have two expressions separated by a comma and building one compound expression. The variables "c" and "x" are of the type **char**. In the first expression "x" is assigned the value of "c." In the second one "c" receives a new value from the keyboard. That makes the final value of "c" different from the value of "x." Actually, the value of the entire expression is the final value of "c."

Try the following program to display the value of compound expressions.

```
/*   Figure 4-6    */
#include <stdio.h>
main()
{
    char x, c='B';
    printf("\nThe value of the expression is: %c",(x=c, c=getchar() ));
    printf("\nThe value of the variable \"x\" is: %c",x);
}
```

If you enter a letter like C in response to the function **getchar,** you get the result:

```
The value of the expression is: C
The value of the variable "x" is: B
```

THE sizeof OPERATOR   The **sizeof** operator is used to return the size in bytes of its operand. It is used in the form:

```
sizeof(b)
```

where:

b   is a variable or a type.

You are free to assign the value of the expression to an integer variable, or to use it directly.

The following program demonstrates using the **sizeof** operator to display the sizes of the different types in bytes (remember that one byte is equal to eight bits).

```
/*   Figure 4-7    */
#include <stdio.h>
main( )
{
    printf("\nThe Size of char is %d ",sizeof(char));
    printf("\nThe Size of int is %d ",sizeof(int));
    printf("\nThe Size of short is %d ",sizeof(short));
    printf("\nThe Size of float is %d ",sizeof(float));
    printf("\nThe Size of long is %d ",sizeof(long));
    printf("\nThe Size of double is %d ",sizeof(double));
    printf("\nThe Size of long double is %d ",sizeof(long double));
}
```

The output is:

```
The Size of char is 1
The Size of int is 2
The Size of short is 2
The Size of float is 4
The Size of long is 4
The Size of double is 8
The Size of long double is 10
```

The next example demonstrates the same idea, but using declared variables instead of types.

```
/*   Figure 4-8    */
#include <stdio.h>
main( )
{
    char a;
int b;  short c;  float d;  long e;
    double f;  long double g;
    printf("\nThe Size of char is %d ",sizeof(a));
    printf("\nThe Size of int is %d ",sizeof(b));
    printf("\nThe Size of short is %d ",sizeof(c));
    printf("\nThe Size of float is %d ",sizeof(d));
    printf("\nThe Size of long is %d ",sizeof(e));
    printf("\nThe Size of double is %d ",sizeof(f));
    printf("\nThe Size of long double is %d ",sizeof(g));
}
```

The output is:

```
The Size of char is 1
The Size of int is 2
The Size of short is 2
The Size of float is 4
The Size of long is 4
The Size of double is 8
The Size of long double is 10
```

If the declared variable is an array, the **sizeof** function will return the size of the array, as shown in the following example:

```
/*   Figure 4-9   */
#include <stdio.h>
main( )
{
    char a[25];
    printf("\nThe Size of the array is %d ",sizeof(a));
}
```

The output of the program is:

```
The Size of the array is 25
```

4-7 BITWISE OPERATORS

Using **C**, you can have access to every bit in memory, thus performing very low-level operations. It is not the major goal of this book to go through low-level operations. However, in order to taste the flavor of the bitwise operators, let us consider the *SHIFT* operations.

THE RIGHT SHIFT OPERATOR   You know that the number 8 is represented in binary as:

```
00001000
```

while the number 4 is represented as:

```
00000100
```

The only difference is that the "1" in the last number is shifted to the right by one bit. If the variable "a" holds the value "8" then you can shift it to the right using the operator **>>** as follows:

```
a >> 1
```

This expression is evaluated as "4." You can shift the number by several bits. For example, you can change "8" into "2" by shifting the number two bits using the expression:

```
a >> 2
```

In general, the right shift operator is used in the form:

```
variable >> number-of-bits
```

Run the following program to demonstrate this operation.

```
/*    Figure 4-9    */
#include <stdio.h>
main()
{
    int a=8;
    printf("\nThe original number is %d",a);
    printf("\nThe number shifted one bit to the right is %d",a>>1);
    printf("\nThe number shifted two bits to the right is %d",a>>2);
}
```

The output is:

```
The original number is 8
The number shifted one bit to the right is 4
The number shifted two bits to the right is 2
```

THE LEFT SHIFT OPERATOR This is the opposite of the right shift operator, as it shifts the number to the left a specified number of bits. The expression takes the form:

```
variable << number-of-bits
```

The following example demonstrates the use of the left shift operator. This time, the shifted values are assigned to variables.

```
/*    Figure 4-10    */
#include <stdio.h>
main()
{
    int a,b,c,d;
    a=1;
    b=a<<1;
    c=a<<2;
    d=a<<3;
    printf("\nThe original number is %d",a);
    printf("\nThe number shifted one bit to the left is %d",b);
    printf("\nThe number shifted two bits to the left is %d",c);
    printf("\nThe number shifted three bits to the left is %d",d);
}
```

The output is:

```
The original number is 1
The number shifted one bit to the left is 2
The number shifted two bits to the left is 4
The number shifted three bits to the left is 8
```

Table 4-5 shows the bitwise operators and their meanings. You may wish to try them to taste more of their flavor.

Table 4-5   Bitwise Operators

Bitwise Operator	Action
&	AND
|	OR
^	XOR
~	One's complement.
>>	Right shift
<<	Left shift

PRECEDENCE OF BITWISE OPERATORS   All of the bitwise operators are evaluated from left to right and their relative precedence is shown in Table 4-6.

Table 4-6   Precedence of Bitwise Operators

Bitwise Operator	Associativity	Precedence
~	From left to right	Highest
<< >>	From left to right	
&	From left to right	
^	From left to right	
|	From left to right	Lowest

4-8 PRECEDENCE OF C OPERATORS

Finally, Table 4-7 shows the precedence and associativity of all the C operators. Only two operators in the table ("–>" and ".") have not been discussed yet, as they belong to *structures*.

Some operators can be confusing, as they use the same characters (for example, the * and the & operators). There is, however, a rule to get you out of this confusion. The *unary operators* (operators with one operand only such as * in "*salary") are of higher precedence than the *binary operators* (operators with two operands such as * in "a*b"). Apply this rule for the following pairs:

- The minus sign operator (unary)
- The subtraction operator (binary)

*	The indirection operator (unary)
*	The multiplication operator (binary)
&	The address-of operator (unary)
&	The bitwise AND operator (binary)

This helps to distinguish between the operators using the same characters. Remember also that when two operators have the same precedence they are evaluated according to their associativity.

Table 4-7   Precedence of C Operators

Operator	Associativity	Precedence
() [] -> .	Left to right	Highest
! ~ ++ -- -		
& * (typecast) sizeof	Right to left	
* / %	Left to right	
+ -	Left to right	
<< >>	Left to right	
< <= > >=	Left to right	
== !=	Left to right	
&	Left to right	
^	Left to right	
|	Left to right	
&&	Left to right	
||	Left to right	
?:	Left to right	
= += -= *= /=	Right to left	
,	Left to right	Lowest

SUMMARY

After this chapter you know almost everything about C operators, the major tool in building C expressions. Their classification, associativity, and precedence are all summarized in tables, so you can easily refer to them when you work with applications in the next chapters. You know also some C shortcuts based on smart operators such as "++" and "+=." Now you are ready for real applications.

Chapter Five

DECISIONS

5-1 MAKING DECISIONS

So far, each of the programs in this book has been a series of instructions executed sequentially one after the other. In real-life applications, however, you will usually need to change the sequence of execution according to specified conditions. Sometimes you need to use a simple condition like:

"**If** it is cold then put your coat on."

In this statement the result action is taken if the condition is evaluated TRUE (the weather is cold). The conditions could be multiple, like those in the following conversation:

"Ok then, **if** I come back early from work, I'll see you tonight; **else if** it is too late I'll make it tomorrow; **else if** my brother arrives tomorrow we can get together on tuesday; **else if** tuesday is a holiday then let it be wednesday; **else** I'll call you to arrange for the next meeting!"

Actually, your program can easily handle such chained or nested conditions as long as you write the adequate code.

In **C** there are many *control structures* used to handle conditions and the resultant decisions. You have been shown before how to express conditions using the conditional operator (**?**). In this chapter you are introduced to more powerful tools: the **if-else** and **switch** constructs.

5-2 THE SIMPLE if STATEMENT

A simple condition is expressed in the form:

```
if (condition)
    statement;
```

It starts with the keyword **if,** followed by a condition (a relational or a logical expression) enclosed in parentheses, followed by the result statement. The statement is executed if the condition is evaluated as TRUE, for example:

```
if (a<100)
    printf("\nThe variable a is less then 100");
```

If the value of "a" is less than "100," the message is displayed on the screen; otherwise, the statement is skipped.

In the following program a credit card limit is tested for a certain purchase. The value of the variable "amount" is received from the keyboard, then tested using the **if** statement. If the condition is TRUE (i.e., the "amount" is less than or equal to 1000), the message "your charge is accepted" is displayed. If the condition is FALSE, the program ends without response.

```
/*   Figure 5-1   */
#include <stdio.h>
main()
{
    float amount;
    printf("\nEnter the amount:");
    scanf("%f",&amount);
    if (amount <= 1000)
       printf("\nYour charge is accepted.");
}
```

The **if** statement is written in two lines just for readability, but it is a single statement ending with a semicolon, and there is no obligation to leave extra spaces.

In the following example another simple condition is added to deal with the other case (i.e., the "amount" is greater than 1000). The message "The amount exceeds your credit limit" appears on the screen in this case.

```
/*   Figure 5-2   */
#include <stdio.h>
main()
{
    float amount;
    printf("\nEnter the amount");
    scanf("%f",&amount);
    if (amount <= 1000)
```

```
        printf("\nYour charge is accepted.");
    if (amount > 1000)
        printf("\nThe amount exceeds your credit limit.");
}
```

You can use more than one statement as a result of one condition by embedding the statements in a block (between braces { }). Look at this example:

```
/*   Figure 5-3    */
#include <stdio.h>
#include <stdlib.h>
main()
{
    float amount;
    printf("\nEnter the amount: ");
    scanf("%f",&amount);
    if (amount <= 1000) {
        printf("\nYour charge is accepted.");
        printf("\nYour price plus taxes is $%.2f",amount*(1.05));
        printf("\nThank you for using C credit card.");
        exit(0);
    }
    printf("\nThe amount exceeds your credit limit.");
}
```

In this example, if the condition is true, the statements inside the block are executed up to the statement **exit(0)**. The function **exit,** which is found in the header file **stdlib.h,** is used to terminate the execution of the program at this point. In this case you do not need the second condition, because if the condition is FALSE the control will be transferred to the last statement, skipping the **if** block. If you enter an amount like 150, the output will be:

```
Enter the amount: 150
Your charge is accepted.
Your price plus taxes is $157.50
Thank you for using C credit card.
```

If you enter a number like 4000 the output will be:

```
Enter the amount: 4000
The amount exceeds your credit limit.
```

Notice that there are no restrictions on the positions of the braces. You may put them anywhere around the block, but arranging the braces in this specific manner, as shown, is a convention for the convenience of the reader. It will help you read your programs, especially when they get larger and contain many nested blocks.

TIP

You may write an **if**-statement, by mistake, like this:

```
if (a>b);
    printf("The charge is accepted");
```

The extra semicolon after the condition will end the statement at this point, and the next statement will be always executed. So, watch your semicolons.

5-3 THE COMPLETE if-else STRUCTURE

You can include the two results of the condition (TRUE and FALSE) in one construct by using the complete **if-else** structure, which takes the form:

```
if (condition)
    statement-1;
else
    statement-2;
```

In this form the body of the condition structure is separated from the rest of the program. When the condition is evaluated, one of the two result statements will be executed, then the program resumes its original flow.

Now you can modify example 5-2 as follows:

```
/*    Figure 5-4    */
#include <stdio.h>
main()
{
    int amount;
    printf("\nEnter the amount: ");
    scanf("%d",&amount);
    if (amount >= 1000)
        printf("\nYour charge is accepted.");
    else
        printf("\nThe amount exceeds your credit limit.");
}
```

Using blocks makes it possible to use many statements as results for either the TRUE or FALSE conditions. The **if-else** structure will then take the form:

```
if (condition) {
    statement(s);
}
else {
    statement(s);
}
```

Look at the following example:

```
/*   Figure 5-5   */
#include <stdio.h>
main()
{
    float amount;
    printf("\nEnter the amount: ");
    scanf("%f",&amount);
    if (amount <= 1000) {
        printf("\nYour charge is accepted.");
        printf("\nYour price plus taxes is $%.2f",amount*(1.05));
    }
    else {
        printf("\nThe amount of purchase exceeds your credit limit.");
        printf("\nSorry, the purchase can\'t be approved.");
    }
    printf("\nThank you for using C credit card.");
    printf("\nWe look forward to doing business with you in the future.");
}
```

If you enter an amount like 100 the output will be:

```
Enter the amount: 100
Your charge is accepted.
Your price plus taxes is $105.00
Thank you for using C credit card.
We look forward to doing business with you in the future.
```

If you enter an amount that exceeds the credit limit like 2000, you will notice that the last two statements in the program are still executed, as they are outside the condition blocks.

This is another run of the program:

```
Enter the amount: 2000
The amount of purchase exceeds your credit limit.
Sorry, the purchase can't be approved.
Thank you for using C credit card.
We look forward to doing business with you in the future.
```

DRILL 5-1

Look at this **if-else**:

```
if (a=5)
    printf("\nThe condition is TRUE");
else
    printf("\nThe condition is FALSE");
```

There is a mistake in the program code that causes the execution of the first **printf** statement all the time, regardless of the value of "a." Can you locate the error?

5-4 NESTING CONDITIONS

The **if-else** construct may contain other **if** or **if-else** constructs, a feature called *nesting*. You must be careful, in this case, as you have to keep track of the different **if**s and the corresponding **else**s. Consider this simple example:

```
if (a>=4)
    if (b>=4)
        printf("result #1");
    else
        printf("result #2");
```

The rule is that every **else** belongs to the last **if** in the same block. In this example the **else** belongs to the second **if**. You can, however, associate it with the first **if** by using a block as follows:

```
if (a>=4) {
    if (b>=4)
        printf("result #1");
}
else
    printf("result #2");
```

This way, the **else** belongs to the first **if**, which is now the closest **if** in the same block.

5-5 THE if-else-if LADDER

The conditions and their associated statements can be arranged in a construct that takes the form:

```
if (condition-1)
    statement-1;
else if (condition-2)
    statement-2;
else if (condition-3)
    statement-3;
...
else
    statement-n;
```

The different conditions are evaluated from the top down, and whenever a condition is evaluated as TRUE, the corresponding statement(s) are executed and the rest of the construct is skipped. This construct is referred to as the **if-else-if** ladder. To demonstrate the use of the ladder consider this example. Suppose that you want to test the ASCII code of a received character to check if it is an alphabetic character. If it is so, you would like to check if it is lowercase or uppercase. Knowing that the ASCII codes for the uppercase letters are in the range 65-90, and those for the lowercase letters are in the range 97-122 (see appendix A), you may use logic as follows:

1. If the code is greater than 64 AND less than 91 then the character is an uppercase letter.

2. If the code is greater than 96 AND less than 123 then the character is a lowercase letter.

3. Other than that, the code does not represent an alphabetic character.

The following program puts this logic into action.

```
/*   Figure 5-6    */
#include <stdio.h>
#include <conio.h>
#include <stdlib.h>
main()
{
    char a;
    printf("\nPlease enter an alphabetic character: ");
    a=getche();
    if (a>64 && a<91)
        printf("\nThe character is an uppercase letter");
    else if (a>96 && a<123)
        printf("\nThe character is a lowercase letter");
    else
        printf("\nThis is not an alphabetic character!");
}
```

The following are sample runs for the program:

```
Please enter an alphabetic character: a     ----> Enter "a"
The character is a lowercase letter
Please enter an alphabetic character: Z     ----> Enter "Z"
The character is an uppercase letter
Please enter an alphabetic character: [     ----> Enter "["
This is not an alphabetic character!
```

DRILL 5-2

Test the following conditions. Which is evaluated as TRUE?

1. (51 > 10)   2. ('A' < 'Z')   3. (38)
4. (!0)   5. (0)   6. (!38)

5-6 THE goto STATEMENT

The **goto** statement is used to transfer the control of the program from one point to another. It is sometimes referred to as unconditional branching.

If the **goto** statement were to be taken out of the **BASIC** language, many programmers would not be able to do without it. In **C**, however, you rarely find the **goto** statement in a program. It is in the language, but is not recommended for a well-structured program. However, it may be useful sometimes in escaping from many levels of nesting in one jump. The **goto** is used in the form:

goto label;

The label is a valid **C** identifier followed by a colon. You can precede any statement by a label in the form:

label: statement;

You can, for example, make a loop in the previous example to repeat the program execution infinitely. This is done by adding a **goto** statement and a label, as in Figure 5-7. In this example we use the label "START:" at the very beginning. The last statement in the program is:

goto START;

Here, the label is written without the colon. Now when the program ends, it starts again. It is important to include a condition that lets you out from the infinite loop caused by the **goto** statement. The program will not stop unless you enter the character "0," and the function **exit** terminates the program.

```
/*      Figure 5-7      */
#include <stdio.h>
#include <conio.h>
#include <stdlib.h>
main()
{
       char a;
START: printf("\n\nPlease enter an alphabetic character: ");
       a=getche();
       if (a=='0')
          exit(0);
       else if (a>64 && a<91)
          printf("\nThe character is an uppercase letter");
       else if (a>96 && a<123)
          printf("\nThe character is a lowercase letter");
       else
```

```
        printf("\nThis is not an alphabetic character!");
        goto START;
}
```

The following is sample run of the program:

```
Please enter an alphabetic character: y
The character is a lowercase letter
Please enter an alphabetic character: U
The character is an uppercase letter
Please enter an alphabetic character: 7
This is not an alphabetic character!
Please enter an alphabetic character: 0 ----> Enter 0 to terminate.
```

The argument of the function **exit** is not of any importance. Usually it is **(0)** if the exit is normal, while with errors the argument **(1)** is used. It is also possible to use the function without any argument.

5-7 TIPS ON USER INPUT

We mentioned in Chapter Two that the **scanf** function is not recommended for string input. Actually, it has some pitfalls when used with characters, too. Although it is reliable for numeric value input, many programmers avoid using it for user input at all. Instead, the user input is always entered as a string and then converted, if required, to a number. The **scanf** function is used most successfully for machine-formatted input.

PITFALLS OF CHARACTER INPUT   You may want to see some of the difficulties encountered with the **scanf** function. Replace the function **getche** in the previous example with the function **scanf**, as shown in the following program, and try to test it.

```
/*      Figure 5-8      */
#include <stdio.h>
#include <stdlib.h>
/* problems encountered with using scanf for user input */
main()
{
        char a;
START:  printf("\n\nPlease enter an alphabetic character: ");
        scanf("%c",&a);
        if (a=='0')
            exit(0);
        else if (a>64 && a<91)
            printf("\nThe character is an uppercase letter");
        else if (a>96 && a<123)
            printf("\nThe character is a lowercase letter");
        else
            printf("\nThis is not an alphabetic character!");
        goto START;
}
```

A sample run of this program gives the following output:

```
Please enter an alphabetic character: A
The character is an uppercase letter    ----> The first message
Please enter an alphabetic character:
This is not an alphabetic character!    ----> The second message
Please enter an alphabetic character: 0
```

Whenever you enter a character to this program it will display two messages. The first message is the expected one according to the specified condition, while the second one is always "This is not an alphabetic character!" This is because when you press the **Enter** key, you are sending a second character which is not, of course, an alphabetic character. This character remains in the buffer and is received by the **scanf** in the second round. You can get around this problem by using some programming techniques. One possible technique is demonstrated in the following program. The response of the user is considered a string of two-character length, and only the first character (a[0]) is tested.

```c
/*      Figure 5-9      */
#include <stdio.h>
#include <stdlib.h>
/* a solution for the problem of using scanf for user input */
main()
{
        char a[2];
START:  printf("\n\nPlease enter an alphabetic character: ");
        scanf("%s",&a);
        if (a[0]=='0')
           exit(0);
        else if (a[0]>64 && a[0]<91)
           printf("\nThe character is an uppercase letter");
        else if (a[0]>96 && a[0]<123)
           printf("\nThe character is a lowercase letter");
        else
           printf("\nThis is not an alphabetic character!");
        goto START;
}
```

As you can see, using the **scanf** function needs attention. So, for character input use character-input functions.

NUMERIC INPUT AS A STRING   In the case of numeric input you can use the function **gets** to accept the input as a character array, then convert it to a number using one of the following functions:

atoi(string)   to convert from ascii **to i**nteger
atof(string)   to convert from ascii **to f**loat

Both functions are in the header file **stdlib.h,** and the second one is in **math.h** as well.

The following example is a modification of example 5-5 using the function **gets** for input, and the function **atof** for conversion:

```
/*      Figure 5-10      */
#include <stdio.h>
#include <stdlib.h>
main()
{
        char response[5];
        float amount;
START: printf("\nEnter the amount: ");
        gets(response);
        amount=atof(response);
        if (amount==0) {
           printf("\nThank you for using C credit card.");
           exit(0);
        }
        if (amount <= 1000) {
           printf("\nYour charge is accepted.");
           printf("\nYour price plus taxes is $%.2f",amount*(1.05));
        }
        else {
           printf("\nThe amount of purchase exceeds your credit limit.");
           printf("\nSorry, the purchase can\'t be approved.");
        }
        goto START;
}
```

In this program the user input is received in the string variable "response." It is then converted to a **float** variable "amount." If you run the program, it will give you the same output as before.

5-8 THE switch CONSTRUCT

Instead of using the **if-else-if** ladder, the **switch** structure is ready to handle multiple choices, such as menu options. The general form of the switch structure is:

```
switch(variable)
{
    case constant1:
         statement(s);
         break;
    case constant2:
         statement(s);
         break;
    case constant3:
         statement(s);
         break;
    ...
    default:
         statement(s);
}
```

The **switch** structure starts with the **switch** keyword followed by one block which contains the different **cases**. Each **case** handles the statements corresponding to an option (a satisfied condition) and ends with the **break** statement which transfers the control out of the **switch** structure to the original program. The variable between the parentheses following the **switch** keyword is used to test the conditions and is referred to as the *control variable*. If it is evaluated as "constant1," the "**case** constant1:" is executed. If evaluated as "constant2," the "**case** constant2:" is executed, and so forth. If the value of the variable does not correspond to any **case**, the **default** case is executed. The control variable of the **switch** could be of the type **int**, **long**, or **char**. Other types are not allowed.

Go back to Drill 2-3 (in Chapter 2) to complete the menu options using the switch structure. Look at Figure 5-11.

```
/*   Figure 5-11    */
#include <stdio.h>
#include <conio.h>
#include <stdlib.h>
main()
{
     char choice;
     char *a,*b,*c,*d,*e,*f,*g,*h;
     a="
MAIN MENU";
     b="-------------------------------------";
     c="1- WordPerfect.";
     d="2- Lotus 1-2-3.";
     e="3- dBASE IV.";
     f="4- AutoCAD.";
     g="5- Exit to DOS.";
     h="Press the required number:";
     printf("\n%s\n%s\n%s\n%s\n%s\n%s\n%s\n%s\n%s\n",a,b,c,d,e,f,g,b,h);
     choice=getche();
/*  Start of the switch block   */
     switch (choice)
        {
           case '1':
               printf("\nWordPerfect is chosen.");
               break;
           case '2':
               printf("\nLotus 1-2-3 is chosen.");
               break;
           case '3':
               printf("\ndBASE IV is chosen.");
               break;
           case '4':
               printf("\nAutoCAD is chosen.");
               break;
           case '5':
               exit(0);
           default :
```

```
        printf("\nSorry, wrong key.");
    }
/* End of the switch block */
    printf("\nThis is the end of the SWITCH.\nBack to the program.");
}
```

In this program a character is received in the variable "choice," then tested in the **switch** construct. If it is '1', '2', '3', or '4', one of the messages in the first four **cases** is displayed, then the **break** statement transfers the control outside the **switch** block. If the option '5' is chosen, the function **exit** ends the program. If any other number is chosen, the **default** case is executed by displaying the error message shown and the program is resumed. A sample run of the menu program gives the following:

```
            MAIN MENU
--------------------------------------
1- WordPerfect.
2- Lotus 1-2-3.
3- dBASE IV.
4- AutoCAD.
5- Exit to DOS.
--------------------------------------
Press the required number:1    ----> Enter the number '1'
WordPerfect is chosen.         ----> Menu response
This is the end of the SWITCH.
Back to the program.
```

The **switch** construct can be nested, if needed, using the block separators ({ }). In this case, you can include another **switch** inside any **case**.

DRILL 5-3

Rewrite the program in Figure 5-11 using the **if-else-if** ladder instead of the **switch** construct.

SUMMARY

> The boldface, in the formulas, represents the keywords and syntax, while the rest is supplied by the programmer.

1. In this chapter you met the control structures that handle conditions in **C**. The following is a summary of syntax and the format of the different structures:

A. The **if-else** construct:

```
if (condition)
    statement(s);
else
    statement(s);
```

- The condition is a relational or logical expression.
- The **else** part is optional and may be omitted.
- If more than one statement follows the **if** or the **else** keywords, you must enclose them in a block using braces ({ }).
- Other **if-else** constructs may be nested in the **if-else** construct.

B. The **if-else-if** ladder:

```
if (condition-1)
    statement-1;
else if (condition-2)
    statement-2;
else if (condition-3)
    statement-3;
...
else
    statement-n;
```

- If more than one statement follows a condition, blocks must be used.

C. The **switch** construct:

```
switch(variable)
{
    case constant1:
        statement(s);
        break;
    case constant2:
        statement(s);
        break;
    case constant3:
        statement(s);
        break;
    ...
    default:
        statement(s);
}
```

- The control variable may be of **int, char,** or **long** type only.
- The **break** statement is used to exit the **switch** construct.
- Nesting of other **switch**es inside the **case**s is allowed.

2. You also used the **goto** statement to transfer the program control to a labeled statement and to perform an infinite loop. It takes the form:

   `goto label;`

3. You also learned the function **exit,** which is used to terminate the program execution. It takes the form:

   `exit(status);`

   - With normal termination the argument "0" may be used.
   - In case of errors any other number may be used.

4. In addition, you learned some techniques to get around the difficulties encountered with user input.

5. Finally, you learned the following functions used to convert strings to numbers:

   atoi(string)   to convert from **a**scii **to** **i**nteger
   atof(string)   to convert from **a**scii **to** **f**loat

Chapter Six

LOOPS

6-1 LOOPING

In order to construct a loop from scratch, you need the following tools:

- a control statement such as **goto**,
- a counter, and
- a condition to exit the loop.

Instead of that, **C** provides three structures for loops with different features that suit different applications. The three constructs are:

- The **for** loop
- The **while** loop
- The **do-while** loop

6-2 THE for LOOP

The **for** loop construct is used to repeat a statement or a block of statements a specified number of times. The construct includes the initialization of the counter, the condition, and the increment. Its general form is:

```
for (counter-initialization; condition; increment)
    statement(s);
```

Consider the following example:

```
/*   Figure 6-1    */
#include <stdio.h>
main()
{
```

```
      int counter;
      for (counter=1; counter<=10; counter++)
         printf("%d ",counter);
}
```

The output is:

```
1 2 3 4 5 6 7 8 9 10
```

In this example the variable "counter" started with an initial value "1" according to the assignment:

```
(counter=1; ...  )
```

The second expression inside the parentheses determines the number of repetitions of the loop:

```
(.. ; counter <=10; ..)
```

It is read as: "as long as the value of counter is less than or equal to 10." The third part is the counter incrementing:

```
(...; ...; counter++)
```

You will recall that this statement is the same as:

```
counter=counter+1;
```

which means "increment the counter by one." The **printf** statement displays the counter values, from "1" to "10."

You may decrement the counter, but you have to use suitable control expression and initial value, for example:

```
for (counter=10; counter>=1; counter--) ..
```

Here the counter starts from "10" and is decremented by "1." The loop will be executed "as long as the counter is greater than or equal to 1," in other words, ten times. If you use these expressions in the last example the output will be:

```
10 9 8 7 6 5 4 3 2 1
```

THE LOOP BLOCK   You may use more than one statement in the **for** loop enclosed in one block as in the following example:

```
/*   Figure 6-2    */
#include <stdio.h>
main()
{
      int counter;
      for (counter=10; counter>=1; --counter) {
         printf("*");
         printf("%d ",counter);
      }
}
```

The output is:
```
*10 *9 *8 *7 *6 *5 *4 *3 *2 *1
```

You can also increment or decrement the counter by any value using traditional assignment statements like:
```
counter=counter+2;
counter=counter-2;
```

or the **C** shorthand equivalents:
```
counter+=2;
counter-=2;
```

There is no rule for arranging the block braces, but for the purpose of readability, you had better use a consistent convention to arrange them. The tradition is to follow the parentheses by the starting brace preceded by one space, and to put the ending brace under the first letter of the keyword **for**. This principle applies for all constructs in this chapter.

TIP

Notice that there is no semicolon after the **for** parentheses. If you put one in by mistake, then the loop construct will be ended at this semicolon and the associated statement(s) will be outside the loop. It will be executed only once.

INFINITE LOOPS Each of the three parts inside the parentheses of the **for** statement are optional. You may omit any of them as long as your program contains the necessary statements to take care of the loop execution, for example:
```
for (;counter>10;) {
    statement(s)...
```

This loop contains only the condition for termination. The initialization is done before the loop. The incrementing must be included inside the loop block.

You can even omit all the expressions as in this example:
```
for (;;)
   printf("\nHello World");
```

This loop is an infinite one. It is repeated continuously unless you include a suitable condition inside the loop block to terminate the execution. If there is no such condition, you can only stop the repeated loop by pressing **Ctrl-Break** to abort the program execution. Even the statement(s) inside the loop are optional. That means that the following loop is legal:

```
for (;;);
```

This is an infinite loop which does nothing.

As an example, you can add this type of loop to the menu program as follows:

```
/*   Figure 6-3    */
#include <stdio.h>
#include <conio.h>
#include <stdlib.h>
main()
{
    char choice,*a,*b,*c,*d,*e,*f,*g,*h;
    a="           MAIN MENU";
    b="------------------------------------";
    c="1- WordPerfect.";
    d="2- Lotus 1-2-3.";
    e="3- dBASE IV.";
    f="4- AutoCAD.";
    g="5- Exit to DOS.";
    h="Press the required number:";
    for (;;) {
        printf("\n\n%s\n%s\n%s\n%s\n%s\n%s\n%s\n%s\n%s"
            ,a,b,c,d,e,f,g,b,h);
        choice=getche();
        switch (choice) {
            case '1':
                    printf("\nWordPerfect is chosen.");
                    break;
            case '2':
                    printf("\nLotus 1-2-3 is chosen.");
                    break;
            case '3':
                    printf("\ndBASE IV is chosen.");
                    break;
            case '4':
                    printf("\nAutoCAD is chosen.");
                    break;
            case '5':
                    exit(0);
            default :
                    printf("\nSorry, wrong key.");
        }
/* End of the switch block */
    }
/* End of the for loop */
}
```

This way, the menu will be repeated after entering a choice, except for the option "5," in which case the program is terminated.

Notice, in this program, that the long **printf** statement is continued on the next line. You can break any statement outside the quotes at any position. If you have to break the statement inside the quotes you must use a single backslash (\) before you press **Enter**.

6-3 THE while LOOP

The **while** loop construct contains only the condition. You have to take care of the other elements (initializing and incrementing). The general form of the **while** loop is:

```
while (condition) {
    statement(s);
}
```

The associated statement(s) are executed as long as the condition is TRUE. Usually more than one statement are associated with the **while** key word. Look at this simple example, which displays the string "Hello World" four times:

```
/*   Figure 6-4    */
#include <stdio.h>
main()
{
    int c=100;
    while (c<=103) {
       printf("\nHello World");
       c++;
    }
    printf("\nDone");
}
```

The output is:

```
Hello World
Hello World
Hello World
Hello World
Done
```

In this example the counter is initialized to the value "100" before the loop starts. Then the string "Hello World" is displayed and the counter is incremented inside the loop block. The loop was done when the counter did not satisfy the condition:

```
counter<=103
```

So it stopped after the fourth round when the value of the counter exceeded "103." Outside the braces of the **while** block, the word "Done" is displayed at the end.

THE FACTORIAL OF A NUMBER   Another example of using the **while** loop is to calculate the factorial of a number. In the following program the number is received from the keyboard using the **scanf** function and is assigned to the variable "number." The variable "factorial" is declared as **long int** to hold the expected large numbers and is initialized with the value "1." The final value of the factorial is reached through the iterative process:

```
factorial=factorial* number--;
```

This statement is equivalent to the two statements:

```
factorial=factorial* number;
number=number-1;
```

The output is displayed using the specifier %ld.

```
/*   Figure 6-5    */
#include <stdio.h>
main()
{
    int number;
    long int factorial=1;
    printf("\nEnter the number:");
    scanf("%d",&number);
    while (number > 1)
        factorial = factorial * number-- ;
    printf("\nThe factorial is %ld", factorial);
}
```

A sample run of the program follows:

```
Enter the number:4
The factorial is 24
```

DRILL 6-1

Rewrite the program in Figure 6-5 using the **for** loop instead of the **while** loop.

THE POWER OPERATOR   The **C** language does not include the power operator, but it can be programmed easily by multiplying the number by itself several times using a simple loop. You need to know the number, the power it is to be raised to, and a counter to count the times of multiplication. In the following program you enter from the keyboard the "number" and the "power," then the result is calculated using a **while** loop.

```
/*   Figure 6-6    */
#include <stdio.h>
main()
{
    int number, power, counter=0;
    long int result=1;
    printf("\nEnter the number:");
    scanf("%d",&number);
    printf("Enter the exponent:");
    scanf("%d",&power);
    while (counter++ < power)
```

```
        result=result*number;
    printf("\n%d raised to the power of %d is: %ld",number,power,result);
}
```

A sample run gives the following output:

```
Enter the number:2
Enter the exponent:10
2 raised to the power of 10 is: 1024
```

In this example the counter is incremented inside the relational expression using the shortcut:

```
(counter++ < power)
```

You are free to increment the counter before or after testing the condition. If you want to increment before testing, you must change the condition as follows:

```
(++counter <= power)
```

In the first case the counter starts from 0, while in the second it starts from 1.

The power function **pow** is in the **C** library of many compilers and is defined in the header file **math.h**. Its form is:

```
result = pow(base,exponent);
```

All the variables are of the double type. You may, however, use this program as your own function to replace the power operator.

6-4 THE do-while LOOP

The only difference between the **do-while** and the other two loops is that in the **do-while** loop the condition comes after the process. It takes the following form:

```
do {
    statement(s);
} while (condition);
```

This means that the process will be executed at least once regardless of the condition evaluation. In the following figure you see a modification of example 6-4, where the **while** loop is replaced by the **do-while** loop. It gives the same output, but if you initialized the variable with a final value of 103 or more, the loop will still be executed once.

```
/*   Figure 6-7   */
#include <stdio.h>
main()
{
```

```
    int c=100;
    do {
       printf("\nHello World");
       c++;
    } while (c<=103);
    printf("\nDone");
}
```

Now look at the factorial example using the **do-while** loop. The same variables are used and the same logic, except for the different construction of the **do-while**.

```
/*   Figure 6-8    */
#include <stdio.h>
main()
{
    int number; long int factorial;
    factorial=1;
    printf("\nEnter the number:");
    scanf("%d",&number);
    do {
        factorial = factorial * number-- ;
    } while (number > 1);
    printf("\nThe factorial is %ld", factorial);
}
```

DRILL 6-2

Modify example 6-8 to display the number and the factorial together, for example: "The factorial of 6=720."

6-5 NESTING OF LOOPS

Like any structures, loops can be nested. For example, you can include the factorial program (in Figure 6-8 or Drill 6-2) into an infinite **for** loop which ends only if you enter the number zero. In this case, the **for** loop is called the *outer loop* and the **do-while** loop is called the *inner loop*. Look at the program in its new shape:

```
/*   Figure 6-9    */
#include <stdio.h>
#include <stdlib.h>
main()
{
    int number, counter; long int factorial;
    for (;;) {                        /* The outer loop */
        factorial=1;
        printf("\nEnter the number:");
        scanf("%d",&number);
        if (number==0)
           exit(0);
```

```
        counter=number;
        do {                        /* The inner loop */
           factorial = factorial * counter-- ;
        } while (counter > 1);
        printf("\nFactorial of %d= %ld", number, factorial);
    }                               /* End of the outer loop */
}
```

A sample run of the program gives the following output:

```
Enter the number:4
Factorial of 4= 24
Enter the number:6
Factorial of 6= 720
Enter the number:0   ----> Enter "0" to end the program.
```

Notice in this example that the variable "number" is no longer used as a counter, so you can save its value for the result display (this is the tip in Drill 6-2).

The following example demonstrates the nesting of two **for** loops inside each other to draw the graph shown in the output.

```
/*   Figure 6-10    */
#include <stdio.h>
main()
{
    int x,y;
    for (x=1; x <= 5; ++x) {
       printf("\n");
       for (y=1; y <= 8; ++y) {
          printf("$");
       }            /* End of inner loop */
    }               /* End of outer loop */
}
```

The output is:

```
$$$$$$$$
$$$$$$$$
$$$$$$$$
$$$$$$$$
$$$$$$$$
```

The outer loop counts the rows, while the inner loop counts the columns. So, for each round of the outer loop (the variable "x") there are eight rounds of the inner loop (the variable "y"). To be sure, you can display the values of "y" instead of the character "$." Also, you can display the row number by displaying the value of "x."

In this case you get an output like this:

```
Row #1  12345678
Row #2  12345678
Row #3  12345678
Row #4  12345678
Row #5  12345678
```

DRILL 6-3

Make the necessary changes in the program 6-10 to get the following graph:

```
*
**
***
****
*****
******
```

6-6 THE break

You already know that the **break** statement is used to terminate a **case** in the **switch** construct. It is also used to terminate a loop, immediately bypassing any conditions in there. The control will be transferred to the first statement following the loop block. If you have nested loops, then the **break** statement inside one loop transfers the control to the next outer loop. This is the main difference between the **break** and the **exit** function, which terminates the whole program.

In the following program the counter "c" starts from "1" and goes all the way to "1000" while the string "Hello World" is displayed. You can, however, terminate the loop by pressing any key. Then you get a message indicating the value of the counter right after the point when the break took place:

```
"Done at counter value= ... "
```

A new function **kbhit** is used in this program to check for a keystroke. If a key has been pressed, it returns the value "1," otherwise it returns "0." The function **kbhit** is defined in the header file **conio.h**.

```
/*   Figure 6-11    */
#include <stdio.h>
#include <conio.h>
main()
{
    int c=1;
    while (c<=1000) {
       printf("\nHello World");
       c++;
       if (kbhit() != 0)     /* check for a keystroke */
          break;
    }
    printf("\nDone at counter value=%d",c);
}
```

A sample run gives the following output:

```
Hello World
Hello World
Hello World
Hello World
Done at counter value=5
```

You have now experienced the three loop structures. You may use any one of them as long as you adapt it to your application. In general, it is better to use the different constructs according to the following recommendations:

- Use the **do-while** loop when you want the associated statement(s) to be executed at least once.
- Use the **while** loop when you want the associated statement(s) to be (or not be) executed according to an external condition, such as "no data left," or "no key is hit."
- Use the **for** loop when you want to control the execution by a variable or a constant.

6-7 LOOPS AND ARRAYS

You have used the array as a data-structure before, to store a string in a character array (in Chapter Two). Actually, you can store any type of data in arrays. Arrays are useful when you store related data items, such as the grades received by students on one test. It is not practical to store the score of each student in a different variable with a different name. The easiest way is to represent the students' scores by an array, using only one identifier. In this case you may declare a **float** array like this:

```
float student_score[100];
```

This array is used to store the scores of up to one hundred students. The number "100" is called the size of the array. In general, you can declare an array in the form:

```
type array_name[size];
```

Each array-element is represented by an index, for example:

student_score[0]	is the score of Able,
student_score[1]	is the score of Baker,
student_score[2]	is the score of Charlie,
....	and,
student_score[99]	is the score of Zachary.

Notice that the array name must not be separated from the brackets containing the index.

You can use the assignment to store values in the array elements, for example:

```
student-score[3]=88.5;
```

This statement stores the value 88.5 in the score of student #4 (remember that the array elements' numbers start with zero). The best way to load the array elements with values is to use loops; for example:

```
for (i=0, i<100, i++) {
    printf("Enter the score of student #%d:",i);
    scanf("%f",student_score[i]);
}
```

This loop will display the students' numbers and accept their scores sequentially. You don't have to use all the elements of the array. You may, for example, use this array to store the scores of ten students only, but it would be better to save the memory and declare an array of size "10."

This type of array is called a *one-dimensional array*, as it takes one index and stores only one type of information (such as scores of one test). You can extend the array to store the scores of more than one test by using the *two-dimensional array*. It is declared in the general form:

```
type array_name[size_1][size_2];
```

You can declare the students' array as in the following example:

```
float student-score[100][5];
```

The first index ([100]) is the number of students and the second one ([5]) is the number of tests, so this declaration allocates 500 memory locations for the scores of 100 students in five tests. You can imagine the 500 locations as shown in Figure 6-12. The test number is the column number, and the student number is the row number. The score itself, which is the actual data, is the number in the intersection of a row and a column. You can use the scores in the table to check the following expressions:

student_score[0][0]==55.5
student_score[2][4]==66.9
student_score[2][3]==45.1

```
/*    Figure 6-12    */
```

		test number				
		0	1	2	3	4
	0	55.5	60.9	66.5	80.3	70.5
student	1	89.1	77.6	99.9	88.7	50.3
number	2	40.5	67.4	90.5	45.1	66.9
	..	...	...	...	...	...
	99	68.8	87.2	90.4	60.1	60.4

In the following example the array "class" is used to store the scores of one student in six different classes. The scores are entered from the keyboard, then the "sum-of-scores" and the "average" are displayed.

```
/*    Figure 6-13    */
#include <stdio.h>
#define MAX        6
main()
{
    int counter, average_score;
    float class[MAX], total=0;
/* Enter the scores for 10 classes */
    for (counter=0; counter<MAX; counter++) {
        printf("\nEnter the score in class # %d : ",counter);
        scanf("%f",&class[counter]);
        total=total+class[counter];
    }
/* Calculate the average score */
    printf("\nThe sum-of-scores =%.2f ",total);
    average_score = (int)total/MAX;
    printf("\nThe average =%d%%",average_score);
}
```

The following is a sample run of the program:

```
Enter the score in class # 0 : 90
Enter the score in class # 1 : 80
Enter the score in class # 2 : 85
Enter the score in class # 3 : 75
Enter the score in class # 4 : 89
Enter the score in class # 5 : 91
The sum-of-scores =510.00
The average =85%
```

Notice the following points in this example:

1. The size of the array is determined by the constant "MAX" which is declared using the directive **#define**. This makes it easy to change the declared size by changing only the value of the constant. Notice that the constant "MAX" is used in different places in the program.

2. The average is displayed as a percentage using the format command "%%" (refer to Table 3-3 in Chapter Three).

3. The average is displayed as an integer using the cast operator (**int**).

4. The variable "total" is initialized to zero at the beginning, then calculated inside the loop by accumulating the scores in it.

Arrays may be initialized when declared, in the same way as regular variables are. The following statement is a declaration and initialization of a one-dimensional **int** array of five elements:

```
int total[5]={ 2 , 4 , 6 , 7 , 2 };
```

This is equivalent to assigning a value for each element such as:

```
total[0]=2;
total[1]=4;   ...
```

A two-dimensional array is initialized in the same way. The following statement declares and initializes a two-dimensional array of the type **float** which holds the scores of five students in three different tests:

```
float exam_score[5][3]={
          { 80.5, 70.5, 80.4 },
          { 50.3, 70.2, 55.7 },
          { 77.3, 80.2, 78   },
          { 60.5, 66.5, 70.4 },
          { 80  , 88.8, 87.2 }
                      };
```

Each line contains the three scores of one student separated by commas and enclosed in braces, and separated from the next student's line by a comma. The whole array is enclosed in a pair of braces. Actually, the array is introduced in this way only for clarity, but all the spaces are optional except the space between the keyword **float** and the rest of the statement.

This initialization is equivalent to assignments like:

test_score[1][3]=80.4;   (student 1, test 3)
test_score[5][2]=88.8;   (student 5, test 2)

...

In the following program you learn how to print the elements of an array using loops. You start with declaring and initializing the arrays:

1. "total[5]" to store the total score for each student.

2. "exam-score[5][3]" to store the score of each test for each student.

As before, the sizes of the arrays are declared as constants at the beginning of the program. So, the dimension "5" is called "STUDENTS" and the dimension "3" is called "TESTS." Expressive names, even if they are long, facilitate reading the program and revising your code. The program contains two **for** loops. The outer one is for the students and uses the counter "student_counter." The inner loop is the tests loop (for each student) and uses the counter "test_counter." The required scores are displayed using the counters as indexes as follows:

```
exam_score[student_counter][test_counter]
```

NOTE

Quick C allows initialization of arrays only if they are **static** or **external**. If you are using **Quick C**, you need to change the array declarations in Figure 6-14 to:

```
static float total[STUDENTS]= ...
static float exam_score[STUDENTS][TESTS]= ...
```

```c
/*   Figure 6-14     */
#include <stdio.h>
#define STUDENTS   5
#define TESTS    3
main()
{
    int test_counter, student_counter;
/* use "static" with Quick C */
    float total[STUDENTS]={0,0,0,0,0};
/* use "static" with Quick C */
    float exam_score[STUDENTS][TESTS]={
                            { 80.5, 70.5, 80.4 },
                            { 50.3, 70.2, 55.7 },
                            { 77.3, 80.2, 78   },
                            { 60.5, 66.5, 70.4 },
                            { 80  , 88.8, 87.2 }
                                };
    for (student_counter=0; student_counter<STUDENTS;student_counter++) {
        printf("\nStudent #%d",student_counter);
        for (test_counter=0; test_counter<TESTS;test_counter++) {
            printf("\n\tScore for exam #%d = %.2f",
                    test_counter,
                exam_score[student_counter][test_counter]);
            total[student_counter]=
                total[student_counter] +
                exam_score[student_counter][test_counter];
        }
        printf("\n\tTotal=%.2f\n",total[student_counter]);
    }
}
```

The output is:

```
Student #0
        Score for exam #0 = 80.50
        Score for exam #1 = 70.50
        Score for exam #2 = 80.40
```

```
Total=231.40

...
...
```

```
Student #4
        Score for exam #0 = 80.00
        Score for exam #1 = 88.80
        Score for exam #2 = 87.20
        Total=256.00
```

Notice that the student number and the total are displayed inside the outer loop, while the test number is displayed in the inner loop.

SUMMARY

> The boldface, in the formulas, represents the keywords and syntax, while the rest is supplied by the programmer.

1. In this chapter you have learned three types of loop constructs: the **for** loop, the **while** loop, and the **do-while** loop. They are used in the following forms:

```
for (counter-initialization; condition; increment)
     statement(s);


while (condition) {
     statement(s);
   }


do {
     statement(s);
} while (condition);
```

2. You learned how to nest loops and how to terminate a loop using the **break** statement.

3. You also learned two new **C** functions:

   kbhit( )   defined in **conio.h**, and
   pow(base,exponent)   defined in **math.h**

4. Finally, you had a second round with numeric arrays, during which you learned the one-dimensional array and the two-dimensional array. You also learned how to initialize, load, process, and print the array elements.

Chapter Seven

FUNCTIONS AND MACROS

7-1 THE C PROGRAM STRUCTURE

The **C** functions you have used so far (such as **printf** and **scanf**) are built into the **C** libraries, but you can also write your own functions. The modular program is usually made up of different functions, each one accomplishing a specific task such as calculating a factorial or raising a number to a power (you already wrote those functions). The final program structure may look like Figure 7-1. In general, the program contains the main block **main( )** (which includes the main logic of processing), followed by the function blocks.

The program file contains other elements in addition to the function blocks. It starts with the **#include** directives, followed by the **#define** directives (if any), followed by *prototypes* of the functions. The prototype is a declaration of a function used in the program. Then come the program building blocks.

When a function is called, the control of the program is transferred to the function statements. When the function is ended, the control is resumed at the next statement following the function call.

The function may return a value of certain type (such as **int** or **float**), which could be used like any other value resulting from an expression. Some functions, however, do not return values. Functions used to display messages are an example. Also, a function may have parameters (like the function **strcpy(x,y)**) or it may be used without parameters (like the function **kbhit( )**).

```
/*   Figure 7-1   */
#include ...
#define ...
Prototypes of functions
main()
{
    ...
}
function_1()
{
    ...
}
function_2()
{
    ...
}
...
function_n()
{
    ...
}
```

PROTOTYPING OF FUNCTIONS The prototype tells the compiler in advance about some characteristics of a function used in the program. It takes the form:

```
type function-name(type argument-1, type argument-2,..);
```

The function name is any legal identifier followed by the function parentheses without any spaces in between. The function "type" is the type of the returned value. If the function does not return a value, the type is defined as **void**. The arguments (or parameters) come inside the parentheses, preceded by their types and separated by commas. If the function does not use any parameters, the word **void** is used inside the parentheses. Here are some examples for prototypes of built-in functions:

```
int getchar(void);
double pow(double x, double y);
void exit(int x);
```

The first function returns an integer value and, as you know, does not take any arguments. The second function takes two **double** arguments (the base and the exponent) and returns a **double** value. The third one returns no value and it takes an **int** argument.

Actually, the header files such as **stdio.h** contain the prototypes of the built-in **C** functions. You may sometimes forget to include the proper header file in your program, but you still have the program running and may get correct results. This is because if you don't include the header, the compiler will use the default type **int** for the function.

CAUTION

You may occasionally encounter functions written with an old method of prototyping such as "**int** func( )," or without any prototyping at all. The programs written in this way are prone to errors and hard to debug. The prototype helps the compiler to detect errors if the function is improperly used.

THE return OF A FUNCTION The function block usually ends with the **return** statement, which takes the form:

```
return(expression);
```

The parentheses are optional, so you may use the return statement as in the following examples:

```
return x;
return x+y;
```

If the function is of the type **void**, no **return** statement is used. Actually, the main block of the **C** program is a function, and because no type is specified, it is therefore considered of the type **int**. Some compilers (like **Turbo C** or **Turbo C++**) give a warning if you don't use the **return** statement at the end of the main block. You can avoid this warning by writing your main function as follows:

```
main()
{
    statement(s);
    return(0);
}
```

This means that no returned value is expected from the main function. From now on, we are going to include this statement in our examples, so as to avoid any warnings! Another way to avoid the warning message is to use the **void** type like this:

```
void main()
{
    ...
}
```

You may also run across programs with the main function declared as:

```
void main(void)
```

THE FUNCTION DEFINITION The function definition is the actual body of the function. It starts with the function header, which is the same as the function prototype but does not end with a semicolon. Then comes the function block. Look at this function which returns the square of a number:

```
int square_it(int x)        /* The function header */
{
    int y;
    y=x*x;
    return y;
}
```

Whenever you want to call this function you can include a statement like the following in your program:

```
b=square_it(a);
```

Here, the value of the variable "a" is passed to the function, where it is received as the value of the variable "x." The function returns the square as the value of "y." The variable "b," in the calling function, receives the returned value. Note that the passed variable "x" must not be declared in the function block. In fact, you can even call the function using numerals like this:

```
b=square_it(25);
```

The whole program might look like the one in Figure 7-2:

```
/*   Figure 7-2    */
#include <stdio.h>
int square_it(int);        /* The function prototype */
main()
{
    int a,b;
    printf("\nEnter a number: ");
    scanf("%d",&a);
    b=square_it(a);
    printf("\nThe square of %d is %d",a,b);
    return(0);
}

/*   The function definition    */
int square_it(int x)              /* The function header */
{
    int y;
    y=x*x;
    return y;
}
```

A sample run gives the following:

```
Enter a number: 4
The square of 4 is 16
```

EXAMPLE: A USER MENU FUNCTION   Adding two numbers is, of course, too simple to be coded as a separate function block. Usually, you use functions in order to keep your main program as simple as possible, and leave the dirty work to functions. For example, you may design a function to display several lines of text which are used more than once, such as a menu text. Take a look at this program:

```
/*   Figure 7-3    */
#include <stdio.h>
#include <conio.h>
void print_menu(void);        /* The function prototype */
main()
{
    int option;
    print_menu();
    option=getche();
    printf("\nYour option is: %c",option);
    return(0);
}

/*   The function definition    */
void print_menu(void)         /* The function header */
{
    printf("\n\t\tMain Menu\n");
    printf("\n1-Add records to the file.");
    printf("\n2-Remove records from the file.");
    printf("\n3-Update a record.");
    printf("\n4-Display records.");
    printf("\n5-Exit the program.");
    printf("\n\nPress the required number:");
}
```

As you can see, using the "print_menu( )" function here saves writing many lines of code in the **main** function. Moreover, you can display the menu at any time just by saying:

```
print_menu();
```

The execution of the program looks like this:

```
        Main Menu
1-Add records to the file.
2-Remove records from the file.
3-Update a record.
4-Display records.
5-Exit the program.

Press the required number:1
Your option is: 1
```

EXAMPLE: THE FACTORIAL FUNCTION
The factorial and similar programs may be needed in many larger applications, so it would be better to write them as functions that can be used in any program. The following example shows you how to write the factorial function and call it from the **main** block.

```
/*   Figure 7-4    */
#include <stdio.h>
long int factorial(int);
main()
{
    int x;
    printf("\nEnter the number:");
    scanf("%d",&x);
```

```
    printf("\nThe factorial is %ld", factorial(x));
    return(0);
}
long int factorial(int number)
{
    long int fac=1;
    for ( ; number > 1 ;) {
       fac = fac * number-- ;
    }
    return(fac);
}
```

Notice that you can print the value of the function call (factorial(x)) directly, like any other expression, using the **printf** statement.

DRILL 7-1

Write a function "power( )" to return the power of an **int** number. Enter the base and the exponent from the keyboard in the main function and call "power( )" to carry on the calculations and return the result.

7-2 PASSING VARIABLES TO FUNCTIONS

You can use as many functions as you want to in your program, and you can call a function from another function or even from itself. In order to avoid errors when using functions, you have to understand the mechanism of passing variables from one function to another.

THE SCOPE OF A VARIABLE The variables declared inside a function block are *local* variables. In other words, they are not seen by any other function in the program, including the **main** function. When you pass a variable like "x" to a function, you are actually passing a copy of the variable, but not the variable itself. This means that the value of the passed variable can never be changed by another function. Even if you use another variable with the same name in the function, you still have two local variables isolated from each other. Suppose that you tried to change the value of "x" in the function block, with a statement like:

"x=x+2;"

The contents of the variable would only change in the function block but would remain unchanged in the main function. They are two different variables, not one.

On the other hand, you can also declare a *global* variable which is accessible from any function in the program file. The global variable is declared anywhere outside the function blocks. For example, you can declare a global variable "price" as follows:

```
#include ...
void total(void);
float price;
main()
{ ...
```

The variable declared in this way is visible to both the main function and the "total" function. You can modify its value in either one and read it in the other. This attribute of variables, being local or global, is called the scope of the variable.

EXAMPLE: THE "SWAP" FUNCTION   The logic of swapping the contents of two variables is simple. If you want to swap "a" and "b," use a third variable like "pot" to hold the contents of any one of the two variables temporarily. The process will be as follows:

```
pot=a;
a=b;
b=pot;
```

You can put this logic into a generic function, to be used with any program. The question is, are you going to use local or global variables?

Using Local Variables   The following program is a trial to swap the contents of two variables by swapping the contents of the local variables in the function "swap-em." Unfortunately, the program is not successful. There are three **printf** statements that let you trace the contents of the two variables "a" and "b."

```
/*   Figure 7-5    */
#include <stdio.h>
void swap_em(int a,int b);
/* failure to change variables by using local variable */
main()
{
    int a,b;
    a=5; b=25;
    printf("\nValues before calling the function: a=%d, b=%d\n",a,b);
    swap_em(a,b);
    printf("\nValues after calling the function: a=%d, b=%d\n",a,b);
    return(0);
}
void swap_em(int a,int b)
{
    int pot;
    pot=a;
```

```
    a=b;
    b=pot;
    printf("\nValues from the function: a=%d, b=%d\n",a,b);
}
```

The output is:

```
Values before calling the function: a=5, b=25
Values from the function: a=25, b=5
Values after calling the function: a=5, b=25
```

Although the values are swapped in the "swap_em" function, they remain unchanged in the main function.

Using Global Variables   In the following program, the function "swap-em" uses the global variables "x" and "y," which are visible from anywhere in the program file.

```
/*   Figure 7-6   */
/* using global variables to swap values */
#include <stdio.h>
int x,y;             /* Global variables declaration */
void swap_em(void);   /* Prototype without arguments */
main()
{
    x=5; y=25;
    printf("\nOriginal values are :x=%d, y=%d\n",x,y);
    swap_em();
    printf("\nValues after swapping :x=%d, y=%d\n",x,y);
    return(0);
}
void swap_em(void)
{
    int pot;
    pot=x;
    x=y;
    y=pot;
}
```

This time you get the required results as follows:

```
Original values are :x=5, y=25
Values after swapping :x=25, y=5
```

NOTE

If you redeclare a global variable inside a function, you are actually declaring a local variable with the same name. As a result, the global variable is hidden from this specific function. This type of variable is sometimes referred to as a *semiglobal* variable.

Although the global variables sound great, they can lead to errors if not used with caution, because they may pick up values from any function. Actually, using local variables in a function makes it independent and useful with many programs, while using global variables repeals the modularity of the program. There is a better way to change the contents of variables: the pointers.

Using Pointers Instead of passing variables, you can pass the addresses of those variables using pointers. This will enable you to access the actual contents of the variables. Look at the example again, but this time with pointers:

```
/*   Figure 7-7   */
#include <stdio.h>
void swap_em(int *a,int *b);
/* changing values of variables using pointers */
main()
{
    int a,b;
    a=5; b=25;
    printf("\nValues before calling the function: a=%d, b=%d\n",a,b);
    swap_em(&a,&b);
    printf("\nValues after calling the function: a=%d, b=%d\n",a,b);
    return(0);
}
void swap_em(int *a,int *b)
{
    int pot;
    pot=*a;
    *a=*b;
    *b=pot;
}
```

The output is:

```
Values before calling the function: a=5, b=25
Values after calling the function: a=25, b=5
```

In this program "a" and "b" are declared as local variables, but when the function is called, the addresses "&a" and "&b" are passed to it. Notice also that the swapping is done on the contents of the addresses ("*a" and "*b").

This is the same principle used in the standard function **scanf**, which reaches the contents of a variable through pointers.

DRILL 7-2

Write a function "swap_f( )" to swap the contents of two float variables "a" and "b."

7-3 FUNCTION RECURSION

You can freely nest functions by calling one from another, as long as your program contains the prototypes at the beginning. Moreover, you can call a function from the function itself; this property of functions is called *recursion*. For example, we can obtain the factorial of a number by repeating the following process:

```
number * factorial(number-1)
```

In other words, to get the factorial of "4" you multiply "4" by the factorial of "3"; and to get the factorial of "3" you multiply "3" by the factorial of "2." This continues until you reach the value "1." Here is the program:

```
/*   Figure 7-8   */
#include <stdio.h>
long int factorial(unsigned);
main()
{
    unsigned x;
    printf("\nEnter the number:");
    scanf("%d",&x);
    printf("\nFactorial is %ld", factorial(x));
    return(0);
}
long int factorial(unsigned number)
{
    if (number<=1)
        return(1);
    else
        return(number * factorial(number-1));
}
```

Note that, because the "number" is always positive, you may use the **unsigned** type in this application.

7-4 THE DURATION OF A VARIABLE

When a specific module (a function) is being executed, the local variables defined inside this module are active in memory. When the module is done, the variables are removed automatically from memory. That is why a local variable is not visible to other modules. The variables that exercise this temporary *duration* are classified as **auto**matic variables. All local variables are **auto**matic by default, but you can also use the word **auto** to declare a variable such as:

```
auto int score;
```

The duration of a local variable can be changed if it is declared as **static**. In this case it will retain its value between the function calls. This is an example of the declaration:

```
static int result;
```

The following program contains two variables: "a" and "b" in the function "kount( )." The first is an **int** (**auto** by default), while the second is **static**. Both variables are incremented by "1" with every call of the function. Take a look at the execution of the program and notice the value of the static variable "b," which builds up with every call. In contrast, the **auto** variable "a" never exceeds the initial value "1." This attribute is useful if you want to count the number of times a certain function is called.

```
/*    Figure 7-9     */
#include <stdio.h>
void kount(void);
main()
{
      int i=1;
      while (i<=4) {
            kount();
            i++;
      }
      return(0);
}
void kount(void)
{
      int a=1;
      static b=1;                    /* variable initialization */
      printf("\nautomatic \"a\"=%d while static \"b\"=%d",a,b);
      a++;
      b++;
}
```

The output is:

```
automatic "a"=1 while static "b"=1
automatic "a"=1 while static "b"=2
automatic "a"=1 while static "b"=3
automatic "a"=1 while static "b"=4
```

Notice that initializing a **static** variable is not like assignment. Any assignment to the variable "b" will override the retained value from the previous call.

Now, do you think that a **static** local variable is the same as a global variable? Not at all. Although both of them stay in memory, the local variable is still hidden from other functions.

7-5 STORAGE CLASSES

Because variables can have different attributes, you would expect that they are not stored in the same way. Actually, the compiler keeps variables in different sections of memory according to their *storage classes*. There are four storage classes:

- auto
- static
- register
- extern

The words **static** and **auto** indicate the duration attribute and the storage class at the same time.

REGISTER VARIABLES   These variables are accessed faster than any other class of variables because they are stored in the registers of the microprocessor, but not in the memory. You may need to declare a register variable if it is accessed repeatedly, as loop counters are. The declaration looks like this example:

```
register int counter;
```

The number of **register** variables, however, is limited by the number of registers. If you exceed this limit, the variables will usually go to the default **auto** class.

Also, because a register is only two bytes long, you can only use this class for **char** and **int** types.

EXTERNAL VARIABLES   The **C** program modules may be contained in different files, with every file containing one or more functions. The scope of a global variable extends to all the files of the program, but you have to redeclare it in the other files as an **external** variable. This will tell the compiler that the variable has been declared before in another file.

The declaration is made using the keyword **extern** in the form:

```
extern int ssn;
```

In a multiple-file program you can also declare a global variable as **static**. This declaration will limit the scope of the variable to its own file.

7-6 MACROS

You have already used the directive "#define" to define constants such as:

```
#define PI 3.14159
```

You can expand this use to write a *macro* that can do the work of several statements, or even that of a function. Look at this macro that defines the cube of a number:

```
#define CUBE(a) a*a*a
```

If, in the program, you called the macro with a statement like:

```
printf("\nThe cube of %d is %d",x,CUBE(x));
```

the variable "a" in the macro is replaced by the variable "x" in the program and you get the result. Usually, the name of the macro (or a constant) is written in uppercase, but it is not an obligation. You must, however, use the same case as used in the definition, because lowercase and uppercase are not equivalent. No semicolon is needed after the macro, unless it contains several statements. The following program contains three macros. The first one is the SQUARE macro that gives the square of a variable. The second uses the SQUARE macro to build the CUBE macro. The third is the SWAP_EM function written as a macro, including all the necessary statements and the **printf** as well. In the third macro you must separate your statement with semicolons.

```
/*    Figure 7-10    */
#include <stdio.h>
#define SQUARE(A)      A*A
#define CUBE(A)        A*SQUARE(A)
#define SWAP_EM(A,B,C) C=A; A=B; B=C; printf("\nA=%d and B=%d",A,B)
main()
{
    int x=3;
    int a=55, b=44, c;
    printf("\nThe square of %d is %d",x,SQUARE(x));
    printf("\nThe cube of %d is %d",x,CUBE(x));
    SWAP_EM(a,b,c);
    return(0);
}
```

The output of this program is:

```
The square of 3 is 9
The cube of 3 is 27
A=44 and B=55
```

Notice that the macro SWAP_EM uses three arguments, the last one (C) equivalent to the "pot" variable you used before. You can write a macro of more than one line using the regular rules of statements (the braces or the backslash).

Now you know that macros can compete with functions, as they are faster and easier and use generic types. On the other hand, they are not modular. Usually, macros are recommended for short routines that do not exceed one line.

DRILL 7-3

Write a macro that takes the form:

```
ASK(prompt,response)
```

The execution of the macro results in the display of a prompt for the user and receives a string of a maximum length of 40 characters.

7-7 HEADER FILES

A good way to organize your program is to put your prototypes, constants, and macros in a header file (with the extension "h"). Then you can include your header file at the beginning of any program, for example:

```
#include <stdio.h>
#include "my_hdrs.h"
main()
{...
```

In the following example the main function is called "my_file.c" and it includes the header file "my_file.h." When you compile the file "my_file.c," they are compiled together as one file, giving the executable file "my_file.exe."

```
/*    Figure 7-11    */
/* The program file "my_file.c" */
#include <stdio.h>
#include <conio.h>
#include "my_file.h"
main()
{
    int x=3;
    printf("\nThe square of %d is %d",x,SQUARE(x));
    printf("\nThe cube of %d is %d",x,CUBE(x));
    wait();
    return(0);
}
void wait(void)
{
```

```
    printf("\nPress any key to continue..");
    getch();
}

/* The header file "my_file.h" */
#define SQUARE(A) A*A              /* macros */
#define CUBE(A)  A*SQUARE(A)
void wait(void);                   /* prototype */
```

7-8 THE "PROJECT" FILES

When a C program is built from different files, it is usually called a *Project* file (in **Turbo C** and **Power C**) or *Mak* file (in **Quick C**). If you are using the integrated environment of **Turbo C** or **Quick C**, all you have to do is put the names of the different files that constitute the project in a "program list." When you compile or run the "project" all of the files are compiled and linked together to make one executable file (with the extension "exe").

If you are working from the DOS prompt, you will need to compile each source file (with the extension ".c") to create an "object file" (with the extension "obj" or the extension "mix" in **Power C**); then you link the object files together to create the executable file. Some tips on multiple-source-file programs will be demonstrated in the following example.

EXAMPLE: THE SECRET-LETTER GAME Before dealing with the program structure, take a look at the execution so you will know how the game goes. This is a sample run:

```
I have a secret letter in my mind.
You have ten trials to guess it.
:a
Sorry, wrong guess!
Try again:b
Sorry, wrong guess!
Try again:c
Correct. My letter is "C"
You got it after 2 trials
Press any key to continue
```

So, the program checks your guess and counts the number of trials. If you failed to guess correctly by the tenth trial, you would get the following message:

```
Sorry, you used up your 10 trials..
My letter was "C"
Better luck next time.
Press any key to continue
```

This project is called "game.prj" or "game.mak" (on the distribution disk). With **Turbo C** you can use "game.prj," and with **Quick C** you can use "game.mak"; otherwise, you have to build the project from the following source files:

- game_prg.c
- game_fns.c
- hold_it.c

The first file contains the following main function:

```
/*    Figure 7-12    */
/*    game-prg.c     */
#include <stdio.h>
#include "game_hdr.h"
char my_char='C';
main()
{
    guess_it();
    hold_it();
    return(0);
}
```

This file uses only two functions: "guess_it" and "hold_it." The first one is the major function that does the work in the game and is included in the second file "game_fns.c." The second is a generic function that holds the screen until you press any key to finish, which is why it is kept in a separate file. This is the listing of the file "game_fns.c":

```
/*    Figure 7-13    */
/*    game_fns.c     */
#include <stdio.h>
#include <ctype.h>              /* With Quick C use #include <stdlib.h> */
#include <conio.h>
#include "game_hdr.h"
extern char my_char;
int guess_it(void)
{
    char a;
    int kount=0;
    start_it();
    do {
        kount++;
        a=toupper(getche());
        if (a==my_char) {
            success(kount-1);
            return (0);
        }
        else if (kount<10)
            printf("\nSorry, wrong guess!\nTry again:");
    } while(a != my_char && kount <10);
    fail();
    return(0);
```

```
}
void start_it(void)
{
    printf("\nI have a secret letter in my mind.");
    printf("\nYou have ten trials to guess it.\n:");
}

void success(int counter)
{
    printf("\a\nCorrect. My letter is \"%c\"\n",my_char);
    printf("You got it after %d trials",counter);
}

void fail(void)
{
    printf("\a\a\nSorry, you used up your 10 trials..\
        \nMy letter was \"%c\" \
        \nBetter luck next time.",my_char);
}
```

As you can see, this file contains four functions which are all related directly to the game, so there was no need to put each in a separate file.

The functions are:

- start_it( ), to display the opening message.
- guess_it( ), to accept and check the user answers.
- success( ), to display the success message.
- fail( ), to display the failure message after 10 trials.

Take a look at the function "guess_it( )" and notice the new built-in function **toupper**. This function is used to convert the letter received from the user to uppercase. If you entered either "c" or "C," the answer would be correct. This function is defined in the header file **ctype.h**.

NOTE
If you are using **Quick C**, include the header file **stdlib.h** instead of **ctype.h**.

You must have noticed, also, the keyword **extern** used to redeclare the global variable "my_char." This variable was declared in the file "game_prg.c."

The third file "hold_it.c" is as simple as that:

```
/*   Figure 7-14    */
/*   hold_it.c      */
#include <stdio.h>
#include <conio.h>
#include "game_hdr.h"
void hold_it(void)
{
```

```
    printf("\nPress any key to continue\n");
    getch();
}
```

Every one of the three source files includes the header file "game_hdr.h" that contains the prototypes of the functions. It is shown in the following figure:

```
/*    Figure 7-15    */
/*    game-hdr.h      */
void start_it(void);
void hold_it(void);
int guess_it(void);
void success(int);
void fail(void);
```

Note that with the function "success" the variable name was not mentioned inside the parentheses. You may do that.

SUMMARY

> The boldface, in the formulas, represents the keywords and syntax, while the rest is supplied by the programmer.

In this chapter you learned about modular program structure, including how to divide your work into functions and how to use prototypes and function definitions.

- The prototype takes the general form:

  ```
  type function-name(type argument-1, type argument-2,..);
  ```

- You know now that every function returns a value of a certain type (except for **void**). The **return** statement takes the form:

  ```
  return(expression);
  ```

- You also know about the different attributes of variables, such as the scope and the duration.

- You are now familiar with the four storage classes of variables: **auto, static, register,** and **extern**.

- Through the examples, you experienced using the local and global variables, and you learned their advantages and disadvantages. You also learned how to change the contents of variables using pointers.

- Along with functions, you learned about macros, which do almost the same work. You are now familiar with the trade-off between functions and macros and can decide when to use which.
- Finally, with the "game" example, you learned how to divide your program into several source files and use them as one project, and you met the new and useful function **toupper,** which capitalizes lowercase letters.

DAY THREE

Chapter Eight

DATA STRUCTURES

8-1 DATA ARCHITECTURE

In addition to the basic types of data, you are also familiar with the arrays that enable you to refer to a group of data items using one identifier. In C there are many derived data types that suit different applications. These types include:

- arrays
- structures
- enumerated types
- user-defined types

In this chapter you are introduced to these data structures which will help you to organize your data when dealing with real-life applications.

8-2 A FINAL TOUR OF ARRAYS

You have used arrays before, and you know both how to load an array with values or characters and how to print its contents. You also know that arrays may have one or more dimensions. Here are more features that will enable you to use arrays as more efficient data structures.

INITIALIZATION OF ARRAYS In Chapter Six you initialized arrays at the time of declaration, using the following statement to declare and initialize a one-dimensional **int** array of five elements:

```
int total[5]={ 2 , 4 , 6 , 7 , 2 };
```

You also initialized a two-dimensional array of the type **float** to hold the scores of five students in three different tests:

```
float exam_score[5][3]={
          { 80.5, 70.5, 80.4 },
          { 50.3, 70.2, 55.7 },
          { 77.3, 80.2, 78   },
          { 60.5, 66.5, 70.4 },
          { 80  , 88.8, 87.2 }
                        };
```

Some compilers (like **Quick C**), as mentioned before, do not allow array initialization unless they are declared as **external** or **static**. Actually, with any compiler, when you declare an array as **static** it will be initialized to zeros at the start-up of the program execution. In general, declaring an array as **static** cleans it up at the start-up of the program.

You can also initialize character arrays at the time of declaration. For example:

```
char n[5+1]="HELLO";
```

This is an array of 5 characters. The extra element is reserved for the **NULL** character. The compiler adds the **NULL** character automatically to the string, but it is your responsibility to leave room for it. If you so wish, you can instead specify the **NULL** character explicitly, like this:

```
char n[5+1]={'H','E','L','L','O','\0'};
```

If you initialize an array with fewer elements than its size, the rest of the elements are initialized to zero. You can also omit the size of the array, as in the following declaration:

```
char n[]={'H','E','L','L','O','\0'};
```

or even with numeric arrays like this:

```
int n[]={62,66,67,81,69};
```

This type of array is called an unsized array. The size of the unsized array is calculated upon declaration and is assumed to be the number of initializing elements.

ARRAYS AND POINTERS Remember that the array name is a pointer to the first element, and you cannot assign it a value. In other words, if you declare an array using this declaration:

```
int total[5];
```

you can point to the first element of the array using either one of the following pointers:

```
total                    (points to the first element)
&total[0]                (points to the first element)
```

Also, the following pairs of pointers are equivalent:

```
total+1 == &total[1];    (points to the second element)
...
total+4 == &total[4];    (points to the fifth element)
```

Or, you can use the array name to refer to the contents like this:

```
*(total)      is the contents of the first element.
*(total+i)    is the contents of the (i+1)th element.
```

MEMORY ALLOCATION Declaring a string as a character array has the advantage of allocating memory beforehand, which is not the case with character pointers. For this reason, when you declare a character pointer such as:

```
char *name;
```

you cannot accept a string from the keyboard using one of the input functions unless you allocate the necessary memory using a special function. The function **malloc** is used for memory allocation. It takes the general form:

```
malloc(number_of_memory_bytes);
```

The function **malloc** returns a pointer of type **void**, and you can use the cast operator to convert it to any type. For example:

```
name=(char *)malloc(20);
```

This allocates 20 bytes for the string pointed to by the pointer "name." The prototype of the function **malloc** is defined in the header file **alloc.h** (in **Turbo C** and other **Borland** products), and in **malloc.h** (in **Quick C** or **Microsoft** products). It is defined also in **stdlib.h** in many compilers, including those listed above.

If it fails to allocate the required memory, the function **malloc** returns a null pointer. You can check to see if the memory allocation has been successful by using an **if** statement.

Here is an example that receives a string from the keyboard and displays it on the screen. Eighty bytes of memory are allocated to the string, and the check is made using the statement:

```
if ( (string=(char *)malloc(80)) == NULL) {
   printf("\nCannot allocate memory");
   return(1);
}
```

It is best to check the success of **malloc** whenever used.

```
/*   Figure 8-1    */
#include <stdio.h>
#include <stdlib.h>
main()
{
    char *string;
    if ( (string=(char *)malloc(80)) == NULL) {
       printf("\nCannot allocate memory");
       return(1);
    }
    printf("\nGive me a string to display: ");
    gets(string);
    printf("The input string is: %s\n",string);
    return(0);
}
```

If you try this example without the function **malloc**, it will not work.

To make the **C** program portable, many programmers use the **sizeof** operator along with **malloc** as in the following statement, where a portion of memory is required to hold ten integers:

```
pntr = (int *)malloc(10*sizeof(int));
```

If a specific machine is using a different integer size, this code will still work properly.

POINTER ARRAYS   You can take the advantages of both character arrays and character pointers and put them together in a data structure whose elements are pointers to strings (rather than characters). The *pointer array* is declared as in this example:

```
char *string[4];
```

This array contains four elements, each of which can handle a character pointer. You may initialize the pointer array on declaration, as in the example:

```
char *season[4]={"spring",
                 "summer",
                 "fall",
                 "winter"};
```

You may also omit the size as you already did with other arrays. In the following example, the pointer array "season[ ]" is declared, initialized, and printed out.

```
/*   Figure 8-2    */
#include <stdio.h>
main()
{
    int i;
    char *season[]={"spring",
                    "summer",
```

```
                    "fall",
                    "winter"};
        for (i=0;i<=3;i++)
           puts(season[i]);
        return(0);
}
```

The output is:

```
spring
summer
fall
winter
```

You can express the same idea using a two-dimensional character array as follows:

```
char season[4][10]={"spring",
                    "summer",
                    "fall",
                    "winter"};
```

Here, the second dimension has a different meaning from that in the numeric arrays; it means the length of each element. So, this array can accept four elements, each of up to ten-character length.

In the following example, the array "season" is initialized and printed using the name of the array "*(season+i)." Notice that with a two-dimensional array you may omit the first dimension but not the second one, as it tells the compiler about the starting location of the next element.

```
/*   Figure 8-3    */
#include <stdio.h>
main()
{
        int i;
        char season[][10]={"spring",
                           "summer",
                           "fall",
                           "winter"};
        for (i=0;i<=3;i++)
           puts(*(season+i));
        return(0);
}
```

PASSING ARRAYS TO FUNCTIONS One advantage of the unsized array is that it can be used to write generic functions that can handle many sizes of arrays. Look at this example, in which an array of numbers is passed to the function "sort-em" to sort the numbers in an ascending order.

The logic of sorting is well known as "the bubble sort." You simply have the program compare each element to its next-door neighbor, and if any element is larger than the next one, then swap them. The comparison needs two nested loops. The outer loop starts from the first element ([0]) and ends right before the last element ([size-1]). The inner loop starts one step after the start of the outer loop ([i+1]) and goes all the way to the last element ([size]).

```
/*   Figure 8-4    */
#include <stdio.h>
#define MAXDIM 100
void sort_em(int num_array[],int size);
main()
{
     int numbers[MAXDIM], actualsize, k;
/* Entering the size of the array */
     printf("Please enter the number of the elements to be sorted:");
     scanf("%d",&actualsize);
/* Entering elements */
     for (k=0; k<actualsize; k++) {
        printf("Element #%d=",k+1);
        scanf("%d",&numbers[k]);
     }
/* Calling the sort function */
     sort_em(numbers,actualsize);
/* Printing results */
     printf("** The sorted array is:\n");
     for (k=0; k<actualsize; k++)
        printf("%d\n",numbers[k]);
     return(0);
}
/* A function for sorting in an ascending order */
void sort_em(int num_array[],int size)
{
     int i, j, pot;
     for (i=0; i<size-1; i++)
        for (j=i+1; j<size; j++)
           if (num_array[i] > num_array[j]) {
              pot=num_array[j];
              num_array[j]=num_array[i];
              num_array[i]=pot;
           }
}
```

A sample run of the program gives the following:

```
Please enter the number of the elements to be sorted:4
Element #1=9
Element #2=345
Element #3=3
Element #4=22
** The sorted array is:
3
9
22
345
```

In this program one hundred locations were reserved for the array elements, but the actual size of the array is entered during the program execution as the value of the variable "actualsize." Although the function "sort_em" uses an unsized array, the "actualsize" is passed to it along with the name of the array via the call:

```
sort_em(numbers, actualsize);
```

Passing the name of the array means passing the address of the array to the function. Therefore, the function was able to change the actual contents of the array in memory. Using a pointer to the array eliminated the need to create another copy of the array to be manipulated by the function.

You could use an array of suitable size in the function, but this "unsized" function is useful in other sorting operations.

DRILL 8-1

1. In the previous example, replace the statements which swap elements with the function "swap_em" which you used before.
2. Write a function to swap two strings.

8-3 STRUCTURES

While arrays are useful for storing related data items of the same basic type, such as scores of students (**float**) or names of players on a football team (**char**), the *structure* is used to store a real "record" that may contain different data types. An employee record, for example, may contain the name, the department code, the social security number, and the pay rate.

These data items can be bundled together in one structure using the **struct** keyword, as follows:

```
struct employee {
    char name[30+1];
    char dept[3+1];
    char SSN[11+1];
    float pay_rate;
};
```

This defines a *template* called "employee" which represents the format of the structure. This template can be used in the program as if it were a data type. For example, you may declare a variable "employee_record" using the following declaration:

```
struct employee employee_record;
```

Here, the variable "employee_record" is of the type "struct employee." Right after this declaration a portion of the memory is reserved for the variable "employee_record." This variable takes a size of 51 bytes for the following structure *members*:

- 31 bytes for "name,"
- 4 bytes for "dept" code,
- 12 bytes for "SSN," and
- 4 bytes for the "pay_rate."

Notice that with string members there is an extra byte allowed for the **NULL** character. This means that only 3 characters are allowed for the department code and 11 characters for the SSN.

If you would like to get the size of this structure, you can use this simple statement:

```
printf("%d",sizeof(employee_record));
```

You can actually declare more than one variable of the type "struct employee" using similar declarations such as:

```
struct employee employee_record_in;
struct employee employee_record_out;
```

You can process the structure in the following ways:

- Initialize a structure.
- Access the members of a structure.
- Access the address of a structure.
- Assign one structure to another.
- Get the size of a structure.

STRUCTURE TEMPLATES AND VARIABLES   There is more than one way to define a structure template and variables. You may, for example, declare the variable with the structure definition in one step as follows:

```
struct employee {
    char name[30+1];
    char dept[3+1];
    char SSN[11+1];
    float pay_rate;
} employee_record;
```

In this case the variable "employee_record" must come before the last semicolon.

You may also declare more than one variable in the same way, like this:

```
struct employee {
    char name[30+1];
    char dept[3+1];
    char SSN[11+1];
    float pay_rate;
} employee_in, employee_out;
```

You can also omit the structure name from the definition as follows:

```
struct {
    char name[30+1];
    char dept[3+1];
    char SSN[11+1];
    float pay_rate;
} employee_record;
```

Using this method, however, does not let you declare more structure variables other than those declared with the structure definition.

The general form of the structure definition is:

```
struct structure_name {
    member_declaration;
    member_declaration;
    ...
} variable_list;
```

The structure name is sometimes referred to as the *structure tag*. Do not confuse it with variable name(s).

ACCESSING MEMBERS A structure member can be accessed using the variable name and the member name separated by the *dot operator* (.) like this:

```
employee_record.name
employee_record.pay_rate
```

For example, to assign the value "23.5" to the pay_rate you can use the statement:

```
employee_record.pay_rate = 23.5;
```

You can also input and output data to and from members in the same way you do with regular variables:

```
scanf("%f",&employee_record.pay_rate);
printf("\n\Pay rate:$%.2f/hr.", employee_record.pay_rate);
```

If you have more than one structure variable (such as "employee_in" and "employee_out") you can move the data from one variable to the other. For example, you can assign one member to the other like this:

```
employee_out.pay_rate = employee_in.pay_rate;
```

You can also assign one structure variable to another:

```
employee_out = employee_in;
```

In the latter case the contents of the two structure variables become identical.

EXAMPLE: EMPLOYEE RECORD In order to put things together, try the following example that reads the members' data from the keyboard and displays on the screen the "employee information."

```
/*  Figure 8-5    */
#include <stdio.h>
#include <conio.h>
/* Macro definition */
#define ASK(prompt,response)    puts(prompt); gets(response)
/* Function declaration */
void hold_it(void);
main()
{
    struct employee {
        char name[30+1];
        char dept[3+1];
        char SSN[11+1];
        float pay_rate;
    };
    struct employee employee_record;
/* Reading from the keyboard */
    ASK("Employee name:",employee_record.name);
    ASK("Employee department (xxx):",employee_record.dept);
    ASK("SSN (###-##-####):",employee_record.SSN);
    printf("Enter pay rate: ");
    scanf("%f",&employee_record.pay_rate);
/* Printing results for reviewing */
    printf("\n\nEmployee Information:\
\nName:%s\nDepartment:%s\nSSN:%s\nPay rate:$%.2f/hr.",
    employee_record.name,
    employee_record.dept,
    employee_record.SSN,
    employee_record.pay_rate);
    hold_it();
    return(0);
}
void hold_it(void)
{
    puts("\nPress any key to continue..");
    getch();
}
```

Notice the following points in this program:

1. The data of the string members are read using the macro "ASK" defined at the beginning of the program. The macro is actually made from two statements, "gets" and "puts." This is more economical than writing many repeated statements.

2. The extra byte left for the **NULL** character is important with successive string inputs. It reminds you of the number of permitted characters for each string, but you have to watch this number yourself. You might not have realized this importance with the one-statement examples which you used before. If you enter, for instance, more than three characters for the department code, your data will be corrupted because the extra characters remain in the buffer.

3. The function "hold_it" is used to suspend the display to give you the chance to examine the displayed information.

A sample run of the program gives the following:

```
Employee name:CAMELIA SOLOMON    -----> Entering Data
Employee department (xxx):ENG
SSN (###-##-####):434-67-6543
Enter pay rate:23.5

Employee Information:         -----> Displaying Information
Name:CAMELIA SOLOMON
Department:ENG
SSN:434-67-6543
Pay rate:$23.50/hr.
Press any key to continue..
```

If you wish to use the function **fgets**, you must allow two bytes for the new-line character (which is added by **fgets**) and the **NULL** character. Here is the example using **fgets**:

```
/*  Figure 8-6    */
#include <stdio.h>
#include <conio.h>
/* Macro definition. Notice the "sizeof" function used with "fgets" */
#define ASK(prompt,response)  fputs(prompt,stdout);
fgets(response,sizeof(response),stdin)
/* Function declaration */
void hold_it(void);
main()
{
/* Notice the size of the character arrays */
    struct employee {
        char name[30+2];
        char dept[3+2];
        char SSN[11+2];
        float pay_rate;
    };
    struct employee employee_record;
/* Reading from the keyboard */
    ASK("Employee name:",employee_record.name);
    ASK("Employee department (xxx):",employee_record.dept);
    ASK("SSN (###-##-####):",employee_record.SSN);
    printf("Enter pay rate: ");
    scanf("%f",&employee_record.pay_rate);
/* Printing results for reviewing */
```

```
/* Notice that the new-line character is not added to the strings */
/* because the functions "fputs" already did that. */
    printf("\n\nEmployee Information:\
\nName:%sDepartment:%sSSN:%sPay rate:$%.2f/hr.",
    employee_record.name,
    employee_record.dept,
    employee_record.SSN,
    employee_record.pay_rate);
    hold_it();
    return(0);
}
void hold_it(void)
{
    puts("\nPress any key to continue..");
    getch();
}
```

There are some points of this program that are worthy of your attention:

1. Notice the **sizeof** function used with the **fgets** to count the number of characters (bytes) in the input string.

2. Because the new-line character is added to each string, you do not need to include it again before displaying each string.

STRUCTURE INITIALIZATION   The structure can be initialized in the same way as are arrays. You may initialize the structure variable "employee_record" at the time of declaration as follows:

```
struct employee employee_record= {
                "John Martin Smith",
                "DPD",
                "567-89-1234",
                30.56,
                };
```

As you can see, every member is initialized according to its type and sequence in the structure. In **Quick C**, structures can only be initialized if they are **static** or **extern**al. The following example puts this initialization into action.

```
/*   Figure 8-7   */
#include <stdio.h>
#include <conio.h>
/* Function declaration */
void hold_it(void);
main()
{
    struct employee {
        char name[30+1];
        char dept[3+1];
        char SSN[11+1];
        float pay_rate;
    };
```

```
/* Declaration and initialization of a structure variable */
    struct employee employee_record= {
                            "John Martin Smith",
                            "DPD",
                            "567-89-1234",
                            30.56,
                            };
/* Printing results */
    printf("\n\nEmployee Information:\
    \nName:%s\nDepartment:%s\nSSN:%s\nPay rate:$%.2f/hr.",
    employee_record.name,
    employee_record.dept,
    employee_record.SSN,
    employee_record.pay_rate);
    hold_it();
    return(0);
}
void hold_it(void)
{
    puts("\nPress any key to continue..");
    getch();
}
```

The output is:

```
Employee Information:
Name:John Martin Smith
Department:DPD
SSN:567-89-1234
Pay rate:$30.56/hr.
Press any key to continue..
```

POINTERS TO STRUCTURES To manipulate the data of a structure by a function, you do not need to pass a copy of the whole structure to the function. You only need to pass the address of the structure to the function, then it will have access to every member in the structure. You can create a pointer to the address of a structure using the "&" operator. For example, if you are using the structure "employee_record," then the pointer to the structure is:

```
&employee_record
```

Look at this example, where the structure pointer is passed to two functions: "read_info" and "display_info." The structure template is declared globally at the beginning, then the structure variable "employee_record" comes later in the main function as a local variable. The argument of the function that handles the structure is a pointer of the type **struct**:

```
void read_info(struct employee *emp_rec)
```

Notice also that you may omit the name of the pointer in the prototype as in:

```
void read_info(struct employee *);
```

```
/*   Figure 8-8   */
/* Pointers to structures */
#include <stdio.h>
#include <conio.h>
#include <math.h>
#define ASK(prompt,response)  fputs(prompt,stdout);
fgets(response,sizeof(response),stdin)
     struct employee{
         char name[30+2];
         char dept[3+2];
         char SSN[11+2];
         float pay_rate;
         };
void read_info(struct employee *);
void display_info(struct employee *);
void hold_it(void);
main()
{
     struct employee employee_record;
     read_info(&employee_record);
     display_info(&employee_record);
     return(0);
}
void read_info(struct employee *emp_rec)
{
     char pay_string[5+2];
     ASK("Employee name:",emp_rec->name);
     ASK("Employee department (xxx):",emp_rec->dept);
     ASK("SSN (###-##-####):",emp_rec->SSN);
     ASK("Pay rate:",pay_string);
     emp_rec->pay_rate=atof(pay_string);
}
void display_info(struct employee *empl_recrd)
{
     printf("\n\nEmployee Information:\
\nName:%sDepartment:%sSSN:%sPay rate:$%.2f/hr.",
     empl_recrd->name,
     empl_recrd->dept,
     empl_recrd->SSN,
     empl_recrd->pay_rate);
     hold_it();
}
void hold_it(void)
{
     puts("\nPress any key to continue..");
     getch();
}
```

In this program you met a new operator "->" which is used with structures. It is called the *indirect membership operator* and is used to refer to a member of a structure by using the pointer to it. So if "emp_rec" is the pointer, then:

emp_rec->name   refers to the "name" member, and

emp_rec->SSN   refers to the "SSN" member.

Keep in mind that the following two expressions mean the same thing:

```
emp_rec->name
(*emp_rec).name
```

In the second expression you must use the parentheses because the dot operator is of higher precedence than the "*" operator.

STRUCTURE ARRAYS AND DATABASES The structure variable as declared so far can only hold information for one employee at a time, but if you declare the variable as an array, it can hold many structures for many employees, which is the same as the idea of storing students' scores in an array. Look at this declaration:

```
struct employee employee_record[10];
```

This declaration reserves memory for ten structures, each of 51 bytes, to hold the information of ten employees. The members of this array of structures are accessed as follows:

```
employee_record[0].name   (the name in the first structure)
employee_record[1].name   (the name in the second structure)
.....
employee_record[0].SSN    (the SSN in the first structure)
employee_record[1].SSN    (the SSN in the second structure)
.....
```

When you use functions in this case, you already have the pointer to the structure, which is the structure array name. In the following example you create a database for employees that can handle up to 100 structures. When you run the program, you get the following choice menu:

```
1. Add a record.
2. List Employee Records.
3. Exit.
```

You can add one employee record at a time using the first option. You can also display the records that contain information using the second option.

```
/*   Figure 8-9   */
#include <stdio.h>
#include <conio.h>
#include <stdlib.h>
#define SIZE     100
```

```
#define ASK(prompt,response)  fputs(prompt,stdout);
fgets(response,sizeof(response),stdin)
     struct employee{
         char name[30+2];
         char dept[3+2];
         char SSN[11+2];
         float pay_rate;
         };
char string[10];          /* a buffer for input strings */
void menu(void);
void read_info(struct employee *);
void display_info(struct employee *);
void hold_it(void);
void line(void);
main()
{
     menu();
     return(0);
}
void menu(void)
{
     static struct employee employee_record[SIZE];
     printf("\n1.Add a record.\n2.List Employee Records.\n3.Exit.");
     ASK("\n\nPress your option number:",string);
     switch(string[0]) {
         case '1':
             read_info(employee_record);
             break;
         case '2':
             display_info(employee_record);
             break;
         case '3':
             exit(0);
         default:
             menu();
     }
     menu();
}
void read_info(struct employee *emp_rec)
{
     int i;
     ASK("Enter employee number:",string);
     i=atoi(string);
     ASK("Employee name:",emp_rec[i].name);
     ASK("Employee department (xxx):",emp_rec[i].dept);
     ASK("SSN (###-##-####):",emp_rec[i].SSN);
     ASK("Pay rate:",string);
     emp_rec[i].pay_rate=atof(string);
}
void display_info(struct employee *empl_recrd)
{
     int i;
     printf("\nEmployee Information:\n");
     line();
     for (i=0; i<SIZE; i++) {
         if (empl_recrd[i].name[0] != 10 &&
             empl_recrd[i].name[0] != 0 ) {
             printf("\nEmployee #%d\nName:%sDepartment:%sSSN:%sPay rate:$%.2f/hr.\n",
```

```
            i,
            empl_recrd[i].name,
            empl_recrd[i].dept,
            empl_recrd[i].SSN,
            empl_recrd[i].pay_rate);
            line();
        }
    }
    hold_it();
}
void hold_it(void)
{
    puts("\nPress any key to continue..");
    getch();
}
void line(void)
{
    int k;
    for (k=1; k<=30; k++)
        putchar('_');
}
```

This is a sample run of the program:

```
1.Add a record.
2.List Employee Records.
3.Exit.
Press your option number:1

Enter employee number:2
Employee name:Charles Berlin
Employee department (xxx):ENG
SSN (###-##-####):555-66-7777
Pay rate:44.5

1.Add a record.
2.List Employee Records.
3.Exit.
Press your option number:2

Employee Information:
_____
Employee #2
Name:Charles Berlin
Department:ENG
SSN:555-66-7777
Pay rate:$44.50/hr.
_____
Press any key to continue..

1.Add a record.
2.List Employee Records.
3.Exit.
Press your option number:3
```

Note in this program the method used to check if an array element is void of data. The check is based on testing the first character of the "name" to see if it is empty. The condition used to do that is:

```
if (empl_recrd[i].name[0] != 10 &&
    empl_recrd[i].name[0] != 0 ) { ...
```

The first character, if void, may contain a zero (after initialization) or a new-line character (if you skipped the "name" entry). The new-line character (ASCII 10) is added by the function **fgets**.

Storing information in a database is a very important programming technique. A database, however, must be associated with a filing system that saves the data permanently on the disk.

Structures can also be nested, which means that any member in a structure can be another previously defined structure. When you step from **C** to **C++**, as you will eventually do, you will see that the structures have evolved into **classes**, which are the main type used in *Object Oriented Programming* (**OOP**).

8-4 ENUMERATIONS

The *enumerations* (or enumerated types) are used to express special data items that can fit into an ordered series, like the days of the week or the months of the year.

To declare an enumeration for the days of the week, the keyword **enum** is used as in this statement:

```
enum weekdays{mon,tue,wed,thu,fri,sat,sun};
```

According to this declaration, every day in the enumeration will possess an **int** value starting from zero. Therefore, "mon" will contain the value "0," "tue" will contain the value "1," and so on. In the following example, an enumeration of the months of the year "months" is declared and displayed using a **for** loop.

```
/*    Figure 8-10    */
#include <stdio.h>
main()
{
    enum months {jan,feb,mar,apr,may,jun,jul,aug,sep,oct,nov,dec};
    int month;
    for (month=jan; month<=dec; month++)
        printf("%d ", month+1);
    return(0);
}
```

The output is:

```
1 2 3 4 5 6 7 8 9 10 11 12
```

You could program the same logic using constants by defining each month name as a number, but using enumerations is a compact method of doing it.

You may, if you wish, override the default values given to the enumeration elements, as in the following example:

```
enum directions {east=10, west=20, north=30, south=40};
```

The enumeration *name*, like a structure, can be used to declare variables of the same type. For example:

```
enum months vacation_month;
```

After this declaration you may use a statement like:

```
vacation_month=dec+1;
```

This will assign the value "12" to "vacation_month."

The general form for the enumerated data type declaration is:

```
enum enumeration_name {enum_1, enum_2,...} variable_list;
```

To declare variables of previously defined enumeration is:

```
enum enumeration_name variable_list;
```

8-5 DEFINING YOUR OWN TYPES

Using the keyword **typedef** you can rename basic or derived types, giving them names that may suit your application or make your program simpler. Look at this declaration:

```
typedef unsigned long int ulong;
```

After this declaration the new type "ulong" becomes known to the compiler and is treated the same as **unsigned long int**. Now if you want to declare more variables of the same type, you can use the newly defined type as in:

```
ulong distance;
```

You may also use **typedef** with structures, as in the following example:

```
typedef struct {
    char name[30+1];
    char dept[3+1];
    char SSN[11+1];
    float pay_rate;
    } record;
```

This definition creates a new type with the name "record." That means you can declare a structure variable using the new type like this:

```
record employee_record;
```

You do not have to use the keyword **struct** again because the new type "record" refers to the same structure.

SUMMARY

In this chapter you gained the necessary skills to let you build and manipulate your data structures in the most efficient way.

- You have had a final round with arrays and now know about pointer arrays and two-dimensional character arrays.
- You know how to initialize all kinds of arrays on declaration.
- You know also how to allocate memory for a character pointer using the function **malloc**.
- You were introduced to the most practical data construct to suit real-life applications, the structure.
- You now know how to define a structure template, how to declare a structure variable, and how to process structure members either directly or by passing structure pointers to functions.
- You were introduced to enumerations, which help to arrange data that fit into an ordered series.
- Finally, you know how to rename basic and derived types and to define them using your own convenient names.
- In this round you learned the following new keywords:

  struct   used to define a structure template
  enum   to declare an enumeration
  typedef   to redefine a data type

Chapter Nine

MISCELLANEOUS TOOLS

9-1 TOOLS TO MANIPULATE STRINGS

The **C** language provides a number of functions to manipulate strings in different ways. In this section, you learn how to use the following tools:

strlen	to measure the length of a string.
strcat	to concatenate two strings.
strncpy	to copy a string up to a specified number of characters.
strcmp	to compare two strings.
strupr and **strlwr**	to change the case of a string.
strchr	to extract a substring starting at a specified character.

Prototypes of these functions are in the header file **string.h**.

Notice, in the examples that follow, that the type **static** is used for declarations of character arrays in order to clean up the array before any I/O operations.

THE LENGTH OF A STRING strlen   The function **strlen** is used to count the number of characters in a string, including the spaces. The **NULL** character that terminates the string is not counted. The prototype of the function takes the form:

```
unsigned strlen(char *a)
```

where:

      a   is the pointer to the string.

In the following program a string is entered from the keyboard and stored in the string variable "string," then the number of characters in the string is displayed using the expression:

```
strlen(string)
```

As you can see in the sample run of the program, when the string "Hello world" was entered the length "11" was displayed.

```
/*    Figure 9-1    */
/* using strlen() to measure the length of a string */
#include <stdio.h>
#include <string.h>
main()
{
    char *string;
    if ( (string=(char *)malloc(80)) == NULL) {
        printf("\n Cannot allocate memory");
        return(1);
    }
    printf("\nGive me a string please: ");
    gets(string);
    printf("The length of this string is: %d\n",strlen(string));
    return(0);
}
```

The following is a sample run of the program:

```
Give me a string please: Hello world
The length of this string is: 11
```

You may assign the function to either an **int**eger or an **unsigned int**eger if you wish. You can also use the function with a string literal as in the following statement:

```
n = strlen("Hello world");
```

STRING CONCATENATION strcat

STRING CONCATENATION strcat   If you have two strings "a" and "b," you can concatenate them using the statement:

```
strcat(a,b);
```

The output string will be stored in the *destination* string "a."

The prototype of the function **strcat** is:

```
char *strcat(char *a, char *b)
```

The following program demonstrates the use of the function to concatenate the first, the middle, and the last name to produce the full name as one string. The program uses two variables:

1. "string": a character array used as a buffer to receive data from the keyboard.

2. "full_name": the destination character array which will contain the full name at the end of the process.

The process is done in steps. When the first name is received from the keyboard, it is catenated to the variable "full_name," then a space is catenated to it. When the middle initial is received, it is catenated to the same variable, then a period and a space are added. Finally, the last name is catenated to the variable to produce the "full_name," which is displayed along with its length. Note that "SPACE" and "PERIOD" are string constants defined at the beginning of the program. Note also the use of the macro "ASK."

```
/*    Figure 9-2    */
/* using strcat() to catenate two strings */
#include <stdio.h>
#include <string.h>
#define  ASK(prompt,response)        puts(prompt); gets(response)
#define  SPACE  " "
#define  PERIOD ". "
main()
{
    static char string[80+1], full_name[80+1];
    ASK("Enter your first name:",string);
    strcat(full_name,string);
    strcat(full_name,SPACE);
    ASK("Enter your middle initial:",string);
    strcat(full_name,string);
    strcat(full_name,PERIOD);
    ASK("Enter your last name:",string);
    strcat(full_name,string);
    printf("Your complete name is: %s\n",full_name);
    printf("It consists of %d characters.",strlen(full_name));
    return(0);
}
```

A sample run of the program gives the following:

```
Enter your first name:
Charles
Enter your middle initial:
W
Enter your last name:
Parkins
Your complete name is: Charles W. Parkins
It consists of 18 characters.
```

CAUTION

The compiler does not check to see if the concatenated string can fit into the destination character array. It is your responsibility to check the sizes of the arrays, or else the results will be unpredictable.

COPYING STRINGS AND SUBSTRINGS strcpy, strncpy You have already used the function **strcpy** to load a character array with a string (where the assignment was not legal). The prototype of the function takes the form:

`char *strcpy(char *a, char *b)`

This function copies the source string "b" to the destination string "a" and returns a pointer to the destination string. So, the statement:

`strcpy(a,b);`

will make "a" a copy of "b." If you display the value of the function itself, you get the same result as when you display "a."

Another copying function, **strncpy**, is used to copy a substring (a part of a string) to a destination string. The prototype of this function is:

`char *strncpy(char *a, char *b, int count)`

where:

a	is the destination string,
b	is the source string, and
count	is the number of characters to be copied from "b" to "a."

So, the statement:

`strncpy(a,b,4);`

will copy the first four characters of "b" into "a."

Take a look at the following example that receives your name from the keyboard, then prints out the name and the first three characters from the name.

```
/*   Figure 9-3   */
/* using strncpy() to copy a string up to a certain number of chars */
#include <stdio.h>
#include <string.h>
#define ASK(prompt,response)     puts(prompt); gets(response)
main()
{
     static char string[10+1], first_name[10+1], first_three[3+1];
     ASK("\nEnter your first name: ",string);
     strcpy(first_name,string);
     strncpy(first_three,string,3);
     printf("\nYour first name is: %s",first_name);
     printf("\nThe first three letters are: %s",first_three);
     return(0);
}
```

A sample run gives the following:

```
Enter your first name:
Daniel                          ----> Your input
Your first name is: Daniel      ----> The program output
The first three letters are: Dan
```

CAUTION

It is your responsibility to check the size of the destination character array, as the compiler does not make this check. If the string does not fit in the character array, the result will be unpredictable.

COMPARING TWO STRINGS strcmp   The function **strcmp** is used to compare two strings. Its prototype takes the form:

```
int strcmp(char *a,char *b)
```

The function returns an integer value based on the result of the comparison as follows:

The return value	*The result of the comparison*
zero	"a" and "b" are identical
negative integer	"a" less than "b"
positive integer	"a" greater than "b"

The following example accepts the first name and stores it in the buffer "string." It is then copied from "string" to the variable "first_name" using the function **strcpy**. The first three characters are then copied to the variable "first_three." Three comparisons are made:

1. The first comparison between "string" and the "first_name," which will always be successful (zero).

2. The second one, between "string" (as the first string) and "first_three" (as the second string), which in this example gives a positive number.

3. The last one, between "first_three" (as the first string) and "string" (as the second string), which in this example gives a negative number.

```
/*   Figure 9-4    */
/* using strcmp() to compare two strings */
#include <stdio.h>
#include <string.h>
#define ASK(prompt,response)  puts(prompt); gets(response)
main()
{
    static char string[10+1], first_name[10+1], first_three[3+1];
    ASK("Enter your first name: ",string);
```

143

```
strcpy(first_name,string);
printf("\nFirst comparison:  %d",strcmp(string,first_name));
strncpy(first_three,string,3);
printf("\nSecond comparison: %d",strcmp(string,first_three));
printf("\nThird comparison:  %d",strcmp(first_three,string));
return(0);
}
```

This is a sample run of the program:

```
Enter your first name:
Clark
First comparison:  0            ----> success
Second comparison: 114          ----> The first is longer
Third comparison:  -114         ----> The first is shorter
```

CHANGING THE CASE strupr, strlwr   You can change the case of the string from lowercase to uppercase or vice versa using the following functions:

```
strlwr(a);
strupr(a);
```

The first function converts the uppercase characters in the string pointed to by "a" to lowercase. The second function changes the lowercase characters to uppercase. The prototype of the two functions are:

```
char *strlwr(char *a)
char *strupr(char *a)
```

The following example reads a string from the keyboard, then displays it twice, once as lowercase and once as uppercase.

```
/*   Figure 9-5   */
/* using strlwr and strupr to change the case */
#include <stdio.h>
#include <string.h>
#define ASK(prompt,response)  puts(prompt); gets(response)
main()
{
    static char string[30+1];
    ASK("Give me a string: ",string);
    printf("\nLowercase: %s",strlwr(string));
    printf("\nUppercase: %s",strupr(string));
    return(0);
}
```

A sample run gives the following:

```
Give me a string:
This is my first tour of C              ----> Your input
Lowercase: this is my first tour of c ----> The program output
Uppercase: THIS IS MY FIRST TOUR OF C
```

STRING SEGMENTATION strchr   Using the function **strchr** you can break the string at a specific character into two segments (substrings) and extract the string segment that follows the character. For example:

```
strchr("Learn C in three days", " ")
```

This expression will produce the segment "C in three days" which starts right after the first occurrence of the space (" "). The prototype of this function is:

```
char *strchr(char *a, char c)
```

where:

a   is the string to be broken, and
c   is the character preceding the segment.

In the following example you are asked to enter your first name. The program then breaks the word into two segments. The first segment is the first letter and the second is the rest of the word. The program displays the two segments then capitalizes the first one and catenates it to the second segment, producing the same name with the first letter capitalized.

```
/*  Figure 9-6   */
/* using strchr to break the string at a specific character */
#include <stdio.h>
#include <string.h>
#define ASK(prompt,response)  puts(prompt); gets(response)
main()
{
    static char string[10+1], first_letter[1+1], rest_of_name[10+1];
    ASK("Enter your first name: ",string);
    strncpy(first_letter,string,1);
    printf("\nThe first letter is: %s",first_letter);
    strcpy(rest_of_name,strchr(string,string[1]));
    printf("\nThe rest of the name is: %s",rest_of_name);
    strcat(strupr(first_letter),rest_of_name);
    printf("\nLet me write it this way: %s",first_letter);
    return(0);
}
```

A sample run gives the following:

```
Enter your first name:
sally               ----> Your input
The first letter is: s    ----> The program output
The rest of the name is: ally
Let me write it this way: Sally
```

CHANGING THE CASE OF A CHARACTER tolower, toupper

The method used in the example above, however, is not the best way to capitalize the first letter of a word. Using the function **toupper** is easier as you can simply write the statement:

```
string[0]=toupper(string[0]);
```

This takes care of the first letter.

A similar function that lets you change the case of a single letter to lowercase is **tolower**. Both functions are in the file **ctype.h** (in **Quick C** it redefined in **stdlib.h**). The prototypes of the two functions are:

```
int toupper(int ch)
int tolower(int ch)
```

DRILL 9-1

Write a program that capitalizes the first letter of each word in a line of text. This is a sample run:

```
Enter your full name:
sally ann abolrous                      ----> The input
Let me write it this way: Sally Ann Abolrous   ----> The output
```

9-2 CONVERSION FUNCTIONS atoi-ltoa

You have used the functions **atof** and **atoi** before (in Chapter 5) to convert ASCII data (strings) to numeric data. Actually, you can change data from ASCII to different types of numeric data and vice versa using similar functions. Table 9-1 shows the names and prototypes of the most useful functions. As you can see in the table, the first three functions return numeric values and take a string argument pointed to by the character pointer "a." The function **atoi** returns an **int**, the function **atof** returns a **double**, and the function **atol** returns a **long int**.

The other two functions convert the numbers to strings and require more arguments. Consider, for example, the prototype of the function **itoa**:

```
char *itoa(int x, char *a, int radix)
```

where:

x	is the number to be converted to a string.
a	is the output character array (or pointer).
radix	is the base of the numbering system.

The function **ltoa** takes similar arguments.

Table 9-1 Conversion Functions

The function	Converts	The prototype
atoi	from ASCII to integer	int atoi(char *a)
atof	from ASCII to integer	double atof(char *a)
atol	from ASCII to long integer	long atol(char *a)
itoa	from integer to ASCII	char *itoa(int x,char *a,int radix)
ltoa	from long integer to ASCII	char *ltoa(long x,char *a,int radix)

The following example demonstrates the use of the first three functions to convert strings to numbers. The data are included in the program itself by using an array of pointers initialized with the initial values. The three elements of the array are strings, but they take the shape of different types of numeric data. Notice that the string "1.2e4" can be read by the function **atof** as if it were a real number in scientific notation. The execution of the program shows each of the strings and the corresponding number after conversion. When you display the output you have to use the exact conversion specifiers in order to get the correct results.

```
/*   Figure 9-7   */
/* changing strings to numerals */
#include <stdio.h>
#include <stdlib.h>
main()
{
    static char *string[]={ "123",
                            "1.2e4",
                            "2147483647",
                            };
    printf("\nThe string 123 converted to integer:%d",atoi(string[0]));
    printf("\nThe string 1.2e4 converted to a float:%f",atof(string[1]));
    printf("\nThe string 2147483647 converted to long:%ld",atol(string[2]));
    return(0);
}
```

The output is:

```
The string 123 converted to integer:123
The string 1.2e4 converted to a float:12000.000000
The string 2147483647 converted to long:2147483647
```

The next program demonstrates the use of the two functions **itoa** and **ltoa** to convert numbers to binary and hexadecimal strings.

```
/*   Figure 9-8   */
/* converting numerals to strings */
#include <stdio.h>
#include <stdlib.h>
main()
```

```
{
    int inum=127;
    char inumstr[40];
    long lnum=2147483647;
    char lnumstr[40];
    printf("\nThe number 127 converted to a binary string:\n%s",
            itoa(inum,inumstr, 2));
    printf("\nThe number 2147483647 converted to a hexadecimal string:\n%s",
            ltoa(lnum,lnumstr, 16));
    return(0);
}
```

The output is:

```
The number 127 converted to a binary string:
1111111
The number 2147483647 converted to a hexadecimal string:
7fffffff
```

9-3 CHARACTER TESTING TOOLS isascii-isxdigit

The C language deals with single characters rather than text strings. You must have realized that text data, whether organized in arrays or structures, are actually made up of single characters. For this reason it is important to have in your hands the necessary tools for testing characters. In this section you learn the following testing functions:

The function	*used to test if the character*
isalpha	is alphabetic
isalnum	is alphanumeric
islower	is lowercase
isupper	is uppercase
isdigit	is a digit
isxdigit	is a hexadecimal digit
isprint	is printable
ispunct	is punctuation
isspace	is a space
iscntrl	is a control character
isascii	is an ASCII character
isgraph	is a graphic character

Any one of these functions returns an **int**eger value. The value of the function is used as a relational expression which is evaluated as zero if the condition is FALSE or a nonzero value if the condition is TRUE. As an example, the following statement will give the output "Yes" because the condition is TRUE:

```
if (isalpha('A'))
   puts("Yes");
```

The prototypes of this group of functions are all similar, as they return **int**egers and take **int**eger arguments. Here is the prototype of the function **islower**:

```
int islower(int ch)
```

If the argument is of the type **char,** it is automatically elevated to the type **int.** The prototypes are defined in the header file **ctype.h.**

If you go back to Figure 5-6, where you tested the input character to see whether it was alphabetic or not, you will find that the logic of the program was too long. Using the character testing functions makes life easier. The following example is an enhanced version of example 5-6 with more features to test the type of any input character. When you run the program you are asked to input an alphanumeric character (a number or a letter). The program will tell if the input is a lowercase or uppercase letter, or a number. If the input is not alphanumeric, then the program will deliver a message according to the situation.

```
/*    Figure 9-9    */
#include <stdio.h>
#include <conio.h>
#include <ctype.h>
main()
{
    char a;
    while (a != 13) {
        printf("\n\nPlease enter an alphanumeric character: ");
        a=getche();
        if (isalnum(a)) {
            if (isupper(a))
                printf("\nOK. This is an uppercase letter");
            else if (islower(a))
                printf("\nOK. This is a lowercase letter");
            else
                printf("\nAll right. This is a number");
        }
        else if (isspace(a)) {
            if (a==32)
                printf("\nI know that. This is the spacebar!");
            else if (a==13)
                printf("\nOh, this the carriage return. I am out of here!");
            else
                printf("\nNo kidding. This is a white-space character.");
        }
        else if (ispunct(a))
            printf("\nHey..this is a punctuation character!");
        else if (iscntrl(a))
            printf("\nSorry.. this is a control character.");
        else
            printf("\nI am sorry. I don\'t know that.");
```

```
        }
        return(0);
}
```

A sample run gives the following:

```
Please enter an alphanumeric character: A
OK. This is an uppercase letter
Please enter an alphanumeric character: e
OK. This is a lowercase letter
Please enter an alphanumeric character: 3
All right. This is a number
Please enter an alphanumeric character:        ----> Press the Spacebar
I know that. This is the spacebar!
Please enter an alphanumeric character:        ----> Press Tab
No kidding. This is a white-space character.
Please enter an alphanumeric character:        ----> Press Ctrl-D
Sorry.. this is a control character.
Please enter an alphanumeric character: *
Hey..this is a punctuation character!
Please enter an alphanumeric character:        ----> Press Enter
Oh, this the carriage return. I am out of here!
```

You may use the **int** type for input, in which case you need to change the input function to **scanf** and enter the ASCII codes instead of the characters. The codes must be from 0 to 255.

Notice the following points about the character set:

1. The alphanumeric characters are members of the set ['A'..'Z','a'..'z','0'..'9'].

2. The printable characters are members of the character set [space .. '~']. These characters correspond to the ASCII codes from 32 to 126.

3. The graphic character set is the same as the printable set but the "space" is excluded. It starts from the ASCII code 33.

4. The **isspace** function tests the *white-space characters* including the space, the tab, and the new-line character.

5. The control character set corresponds to the ASCII codes from 0 to 31 in addition to 127 (the Del character).

6. The punctuation character set corresponds to the ASCII codes from 33 to 47, from 58 to 64, from 91-96, and from 123 to 126.

7. The **isascii** function tests the characters that correspond to the ASCII codes from 0 to 127, which is the standard region of the characters.

The printable, punctuation, and control ASCII codes and their corresponding characters are shown in appendix A.

DRILL 9-2

Write a program to print the standard ASCII character codes (from 0 to 127) and also print each corresponding character if alphanumeric, or send a message to classify the character according to the following categories:

- control,
- punctuation,
- spacebar, or
- white space.

Notice that some categories overlap.

9-4 EXECUTING DOS COMMANDS system

If you already designed your "menu" program (which started with Drill 2-3), you may be waiting to know how to run programs like **Lotus 1-2-3** or **WordPerfect** from the C program. Here is one function you can use to issue a **DOS** command:

```
int system(char *DOS-command-string);
```

This prototype is defined in the header file **stdlib.h**. The function returns "0" if successful and a nonzero value if not. As an example, you may use the following code to run the program **WordPerfect**. When you exit from **WordPerfect**, you will be back to the C program, and the message "Hello again" will be displayed on your screen.

```
/*   Figure 9-10   */
#include <stdio.h>
#include <stdlib.h>
main()
{
    system("wp");
    printf("Hello again");
    return(0);
}
```

In this program the string "wp" is a legal **DOS** command, which may be a name of a batch file "wp.bat" or the executable file "wp.exe." In either case the directory of file "wp" must be included in the "PATH." You can write similar commands using batch files such as "123.bat" and "dbase.bat." Such commands that spawn other programs from the C program may encounter problems (such as lack of available memory). If you are using an integrated environment for your programs, it would be better to exit it and run the program from the

DOS prompt. You may also need to compile the program using a medium or large memory model.

SUMMARY

1. In this chapter you experienced using important tools to manipulate strings. You learned these new functions:

   strlen   to measure the length of a string.
   strcat   to concatenate two strings.
   strncpy   to copy a string up to a specified number of characters.
   strcmp   to compare two strings.
   strupr and
   strlwr   to change the case of a string.
   strchr   to extract a substring starting at a specified character.

The prototypes of these functions are found in the file **string.h**.

2. For dealing with single characters you learned the function **tolower** as a conjugate to the function **toupper**. They are both in the header file **ctype.h**. In **Quick C** they are redefined in **stdlib.h**.

3. You also learned how to test each single character to classify its category using the following functions:

   isalpha   is alphabetic
   isalnum   is alphanumeric
   islower   is lowercase
   isupper   is uppercase
   isdigit   is a digit
   isxdigit is a hexadecimal digit
   isprint   is printable
   ispunct   is punctuation
   isspace   is a space
   iscntrl   is a control character
   isascii   is an ASCII character
   isgraph   is a graphic character

The prototypes of these functions are found in the file **ctype.h**.

4. Finally, you learned how to issue a **DOS** command from your **C** program using the function **system**. Such a feature enables you to spawn an application program, such as **Lotus 1-2-3** or **WordPerfect**, from a menu program.

Chapter Ten

FILES AND APPLICATIONS

10-1 DATA FILES IN C

Unless you store the information to a disk, every data item you enter into a program will evaporate when the program exits. Using disk files will enable you to save your data permanently to disk and retrieve them later.

A file, in general, is defined as a collection of related *records*, such as the "employee record." Each record is a collection of related items called *fields*, such as the "name" field and the "SSN" field. Each field consists of a group of characters. The common operations associated with file processing are:

- Reading from a file (input)
- Writing to a file (output)
- Appending to a file (writing at the end)
- Updating a file (Input and output I/O)

SEQUENTIAL AND RANDOM ACCESS Data can be accessed either sequentially or randomly. An example of a *sequential-access file* is a purchase list which has to be read from the top down to access a specific item. The *random-access file* is like the boxes in a post office, which are identified by numbers and accessed directly without the need to go through them all.

DATA INPUT/OUTPUT In C, data are transferred to and from files in one of three ways:

- Record I/O (one record at a time).
- String I/O (one string at a time).

- Character I/O (one character at a time).

ACCESS FUNCTIONS   There are two groups of functions in **C** with which to access data in files:

- *High-Level functions*, which support buffered transfer of data.
- *Low-Level functions*, which support unbuffered transfer of data.

The first type of functions are easy to use and portable with different computers and compilers.

In this chapter you are going to use the high-level functions to manipulate data in sequentially accessed files.

FILES, STREAMS, AND PHYSICAL DEVICES   You have already used some functions that write output to, or receive input from, different physical devices (such as **fputs**, **fgets** and **putc**). You can think of **C** files as streams of data that can be connected to different physical devices such as the screen, the printer, or the hard disk. Some connections are predefined as the standard streams (or standard devices). These streams and corresponding devices are shown in Table 10-1. You can redirect the data stream by changing the device name. For example, the statement:

```
fputs("Hello", stdprn);
```

sends the string "Hello" to the printer, while the statement:

```
fputs("Hello", stdout);
```

sends the string "Hello" to the screen.

Table 10-1   Standard Streams

Stream	Physical device
stdin	keyboard
stdout	screen
stdprn	printer
stderr	screen
stdaux	screen

10-2 THE FILE PROTOCOL fopen, fclose

In order to use a data file on the hard disk you must establish a connection between the data stream and the hard disk. This is done by *opening* the file, using the function **fopen**. The function takes the general form:

```
fopen(file_name, access_mode)
```

where:

file_name: is a legal file name (may include the path).
access_mode: is one of the following strings:
      "r"   to open a file for reading only (for input)
      "w"   to open a file for writing only (for output)
      "a"   to open a file for appending (for output)

When the file is opened using either the write mode (**"w"**) or the append mode (**"a"**), it will be created if it does not already exist. However, if an existing file is opened in the write mode (**"w"**), it will be overwritten, while in the append mode (**"a"**) the new data are added to the end of the existing file. The file cannot be opened in the read-only mode (**"r"**) unless it already exists. Adding a plus sign (+) to any of the three modes creates one of the following new modes, which are called update modes:

"r+"   to open an existing file for reading and writing (I/O)
"w+"   to open a new file for reading and writing (I/O)
"a+"   to open a file for reading and appending (I/O) and create the file if it does not exist.

The three update modes permit reading and writing to be performed on the file.

This example opens a file named "phones.dat" in the current directory, for appending:

```
FILE *fp;
fp=fopen("phones.dat" , "a");
```

The function **fopen** returns a pointer to the structure **FILE** which is defined in the header file **stdio.h**. This is why you must declare a pointer "fp" of the type **FILE**. This pointer is called the *file pointer*.

When you are through with processing the file data, you have to *close* the file. Closing the file is important as it writes any data remaining in the buffer to the output file. The function **fclose** is used to close the file. For example, the statement:

```
fclose(fp);
```

is used to close a file pointed to by "fp."

When closing the file, the file pointer is used as an argument of the function, but the file name is not used.

When you open a file, it would be better to check to see if the operation is successful as follows:

- If the operation is successful, the function returns a pointer to the file ("fp" in this example).
- If an error is encountered (for example, if the file does not exist), the function returns **NULL**.

Usually, this is done in one step as in the following statement:

```
if ((fp=fopen("phones.dat", "r")) != NULL) {
....
....
}
puts("Error in opening the file..");
```

When you close a file successfully, the function **fclose** returns a zero; any other value indicates an error.

The prototypes for the **fopen** and **fclose** functions take the forms:

```
FILE *fopen(char *file_name, char *access_mode)
int fclose(FILE *file_pointer)
```

10-3 ASCII AND BINARY FILES

Before you start processing data in files, let us see how the data in a file looks. The sequential file is a sequence of strings separated by the line-feed character "LF" (ASCII 10). Suppose you created a file that holds the names of some friends. You may imagine the file in the memory as shown below:

```
J a m e s   S t r a h a n 10 T o n y   P e n n 10 H i t e   B i l l e s 10
<-------- name 1 -------> LF <--- name 2 ----> LF <------ name 3 -----> LF
```

This type of file is actually a sequence of characters, including the LF characters. When the file is written to the disk it may be dumped as is in memory (in which case it is called a *binary file*), or some character translation may take place (in which case it is called an *ASCII file*). In the ASCII file, each LF character is translated into a carriage return "CR" (ASCII 13) and LF, as shown below:

```
J a m e s   S t r a h a n 13 10 T o n y   P e n n 13 10 H i t e   B i l l e s 13 10
<-------- name 1 ------->  CR+LF  <--- name 2 ---->  CR+LF  <------ name 3 ----->  CR+LF
```

If you display this ASCII sequential file on the screen using the **DOS** command **TYPE**, you will see the file as successive lines, each containing one name.

A binary file is opened by adding the letter "**b**" to the access mode, thus forming the following three new modes:

"rb"   to open a binary file for reading
"wb"   to open a binary file for writing
"ab"   to open a binary file for appending

If the letter "b" is not used, the file is considered ASCII by default.

When a file is written to the disk, an End-Of-File mark (**EOF**) is added to the end of it. The **EOF** mark is a predefined constant of value "–1" (or Hexadecimal ffff).

10-4 FILE INPUT AND OUTPUT

You have already used the function **putc** to write a single character to a stream (**stdout** or **stdprn**) and the function **fputs** to write a string to a stream. Another function, **fprintf**, which is the general case of **printf**, may be used to write a string to a file. In this section these three functions are introduced.

WRITING A CHARACTER TO A FILE putc   To write a character to a file, use the function **putc** which takes the form:

```
putc(c, fp)
```

where:

c   is the character to be written to the file, and
fp   is a file pointer.

Here is an example of a function that writes a character array "item," one character at a time, to the file pointed to by the pointer "fp":

```
/*   Figure 10-1   */
/* a function to write a string to a file one character at a time */
void file_item(char item[])
{
    int k=0;
```

```
    while (item[k] != NULL) {          /* test the end of the string */
          putc(item[k], fp);
          k++;
    }
    putc('\n', fp);                    /* add the LF character */
}
```

The pointer to the character array (item) is passed to the function as an argument. Then, using a **while** loop, a test is made every round to see if the **NULL** character is encountered (which indicates the end of the string). As long as there are characters in the array, they are written to the file; otherwise, the loop is terminated and the LF character is written to the file. This function is used, in the following figure, to write the popular **C** string "Hello World" to a file called "hello.dat" in the current directory.

```
/*   Figure 10-2    */
/* Writing a string to a file one character at a time */
#include <stdio.h>
#include <string.h>
#define FNAME            "hello.dat"
void file_item(char[]);
FILE *fp;
main()
{
    char item[41];
    strcpy(item,"Hello World");
    if ((fp=fopen(FNAME,"w")) != NULL) {
        file_item(item);
        fclose(fp);
    }
    else
        printf("\nError in opening the file: %s",FNAME);
    return(0);
}
void file_item(char item[])
{
    int k=0;
    while (item[k] != NULL) {
        putc(item[k],fp);
        k++;
    }
    putc('\n',fp);
}
```

When you run this program nothing will show up on your screen. However, the file "hello.dat" will have been created in the current directory. Notice that no matter how many times you run the program, the file will always contain one string. This is because you used the write mode ("**w**"). If, however, you use the append mode ("**a**"), you will add a new string every time you run the program.

If you are anxious to see the results, you can look up the contents of the file using the **DOS** command:

```
TYPE hello.dat
```

WRITING A STRING TO A FILE fputs, fprintf   The advantage of using the character-based function **putc** is that you can have control of every byte you write to the file. You may, however, prefer to transfer your data one string at a time. To write the character array "item" to a file pointed to by "fp" use the statement:

```
fputs(item, fp);
```

or, you can even write an explicit string like this:

```
fputs("Hello again\n", fp);
```

The function **fputs** takes the general form:

```
fputs(s, fp)
```

where:

> s   is a character array.
> fp   is a file pointer.

The function **fprintf** does the same work as the function **printf** except that the output can be sent to a file or a specific output device (such as the printer) instead of the screen. For example, you can write the following statement to write the character array "item" to a file pointed to by "fp":

```
fprintf(fp, "%s", item);
```

You may also use the following statement to write the string "Hello there" using the same function:

```
fprintf(fp, "Hello there\n");
```

If you replace the file pointer "fp" with the device **stdprn,** the output will go to the printer.

With functions that write the whole string to the file, you must be sure that the LF character is added to the string before sending it to the file. Keep in mind that in some cases, the string may already include the LF character. For example, if you use the function **fgets** to accept strings from the keyboard, the LF character is added to the string automatically. In this case you do not need to add another one.

The function **fprintf** takes the general form:

```
fprintf(fp, "format", arg1, arg2,...)
```

where:

fp	is a file pointer.
format	is the format-characters string.
arg1,..	are the arguments to be written to the file.

READING CHARACTERS FROM A FILE getc   To read a file one character at a time, use the function **getc**, which is the counterpart of **putc**. It takes the general form:

`getc(fp)`

where:

fp   is a file-pointer.

You can assign the function **getc** to an **int** or a **char** variable as in the following statements:

```
c=getc(fp);
string[i]=getc(fp);
```

In the following program, the file "hello.dat" is read by simply reading each character using the function **getc** and sending it to the screen using the function **putc**. The program contains an **if** condition to open the file and test for any possible open errors. The reading process is done using a **while** loop which ends when the **EOF** character is detected.

```
/*   Figure 10-3    */
/* Reading a file one character at a time */
#include <stdio.h>
#define FNAME          "hello.dat"
FILE *fp;
main()
{
    int c;
    if (NULL != (fp=fopen(FNAME,"r"))) {
        while ((c=getc(fp)) != EOF) {           /* read a character */
            putc(c,stdout);                     /* display the character */
        }
        fclose(fp);
    }
    else
        printf("\nError in opening the file: %s",FNAME);
    return(0);
}
```

This program displays on the screen whatever was written to the file "hello.dat." You can use this simple program to display any text file, by changing the name "hello.dat" to the name of the file to be read. The program actually replaces the **DOS** command **TYPE**.

TIP

If you want to test the effect of the open-error statement, delete the file "hello.dat" and run the program.

In real-life applications, however, a file is not generally read as one unit. Usually, you will want to read one string at a time for further processing and then send it with other items to the output. This being the case, reading a file will usually include other activities beside copying each character to the output. With every read, the program has to check for the LF character so it can find the end of each string. Also, it must check for the End-Of-File mark (**EOF**) which comes at the end of the file. There is an easier way to read a file: reading one string at a time.

READING A STRING FROM A FILE fgets   If the file was written properly, it may be easier to read it using the function **fgets**, which reads one string at a time. The function takes the general form:

```
fgets(s, n, fp)
```

where:

s	is a character array.
n	is the maximum number of characters.
fp	is a file pointer (or a standard device).

You may use the function as in this statement to read the character array "name" into a buffer of up to 80 characters:

```
fgets(name, 80, fp);
```

The function returns **NULL** if the **EOF** mark is encountered. This way, you can read and check the **EOF** mark in one statement like this:

```
if (fgets(name, 80, fp) == NULL)
    return(EOF);
```

The function **fgets** continues to read until either "n-1" characters are read or the LF character is read, whichever comes first. If the LF character is read, it is added to the string.

The following example uses the function **fgets** to read the file "hello.dat".

```
/*   Figure 10-4   */
/* Reading a file one string (line) at a time */
#include <stdio.h>
#define FNAME       "hello.dat"
#define LINESIZE    82
#define DONE        1
```

```
int get_item(char[ ]);
void display_info(char[ ]);
FILE *fp;
main()
{
    static char contents[LINESIZE];
    if (NULL != (fp=fopen(FNAME,"r"))) {
        while (get_item(contents) != EOF)     /* stop at EOF */
            display_info(contents);
        fclose(fp);
    }
    else
        printf("\nError in opening the file: %s",FNAME);
    return(0);
}
int get_item(char item[ ])
{

    if (fgets(item,LINESIZE,fp) == NULL)    /* read and check EOF */
        return(EOF);                        /* return the EOF flag */
    return(DONE);                           /* return normally */
}
void display_info(char name[ ])
{
    printf("%s",name);
}
```

Notice the following in the logic of the main function:

1. The program starts by opening the file associated with the open-error check.

2. A **while** loop in the main function is used to check the flag returned by the function "get item." Inside the loop, the successive lines of the file are read and displayed until the flag **EOF** is returned, then the file is closed.

3. If the program encounters an error upon opening the file, it delivers an error message and exits.

4. Note that the size of the character array is 82 (LINESIZE), which makes the program more generic and able to handle a line of text of up to 80 characters.

5. Notice also that when you use an unsized array in a function, you cannot use the **sizeof** function because the size of the passed array is unknown to the function.

10-5 APPLICATION 1: A TELEPHONE DIRECTORY

You now have enough expertise with file handling to write an application program. Let us start with a telephone directory that stores names and telephone numbers. The program starts with a menu like this:

```
........... MENU ............
1. Add Records to the File.
2. Display File Information.
3. Exit.
Press the Required Number:
```

When you press "1" the program prompts you to enter the name and the phone number, then it writes them to a file. If you press "2" the file is displayed on your screen as in the following sample run.

```
........... MENU ............
1. Add Records to the File.
2. Display File Information.
3. Exit.
Press the Required Number:      ----> Press #2
      NAME:James Strahan
      PHONE-NUMBER:(504) 666-7878
      NAME:Brandon Northcutt
      PHONE-NUMBER:(504) 565-8888
      NAME:Hite Billes
      PHONE-NUMBER:(510) 778-1234
** End Of File **
Press any key to continue..

........... MENU ............
1. Add Records to the File.
2. Display File Information.
3. Exit.
Press the Required Number:      ----> Press #3
```

Pressing "3" ends the program. This program is shown in Figure 10-5. Take a look at the listing, then read about it in detail.

```c
/*   Figure 10-5    */
/* Telephone Directory */
#include <stdio.h>
#include <conio.h>
#include <stdlib.h>
#include <string.h>
#define MAXNAME       40+1
#define MAXPHONE      14+1
#define FNAME         "phones.dat"
#define LF            '\n'
#define DONE          1
#define BUFR          80
#define ASK(prompt,response)    fputs(prompt,stdout); gets(response)
/* define prototypes for functions */
void menu(void);
void write_rec(char[],char[]);
void file_item(char[]);
void display_info(char[],char[]);
/* define global variables */
FILE *fp;
void main()
```

```
{
    menu();
}
/* -------------------   End of main() ------------------------ */
/* -------------------   func. menu     ---------------------- */
void menu(void)
{
    static char name[MAXNAME], phone[MAXPHONE];
    int option, i;
    for (i=1; i<=24; i++)
        printf("\n");
    printf("........... MENU ............");
    printf("\n\n1. Add Records to the File.");
    printf("\n\n2. Display File Information.");
    printf("\n\n3. Exit.");
    printf("\n\nPress the Required Number:\n\n");
    option=getch();
    switch(option)
    {
        case '1':
                fp=fopen(FNAME,"a");
                while (getinfo(name,phone) != NULL)
                    write_rec(name,phone);
                fclose(fp);
                break;
        case '2':
                fp=fopen(FNAME,"r");
                while (read_rec(name,phone) != EOF)
                    display_info(name,phone);
                printf("\n** End Of File **");
                printf("\nPress any key to continue..\n");
                getch();
                fclose(fp);
                break;
        case '3':
                exit(0);
                default:
                menu();
    }
    menu();
}
/* -----------------   func. getinfo    ----------------------- */
int getinfo(name,phone)
char name[], phone[];
{
    ASK("\nEnter name: ",name);
    if(name[0] == NULL)     /* check if the first letter is NULL */
        return(NULL);            /* a flag to indicate end-of-input */
    else
        ASK("Enter phone-number: ",phone);
    return(DONE);            /* normal return */
}
/* -------------------   func. write_rec ------------------- */
void write_rec(name,phone)
char name[], phone[];
{
        fprintf(fp,"%s\n",name);        /* write "name" to the file */
        fprintf(fp,"%s\n",phone);
```

```
}
/* -------------------- func. read_rec  --------------------- */
int read_rec(name,phone)
char name[], phone[];
{
    if (fgets(name,BUFR,fp) == NULL)   /* check EOF */
        return(EOF);
/* return the EOF flag */
    if (fgets(phone,BUFR,fp) == NULL)
        return(EOF);
    return(DONE);                       /* return normally */
}
/* ------------------ func. display_info ---------------------- */
void display_info(name,phone)
char name[], phone[];
{
    printf("\tNAME:%s",name);
    printf("\tPHONE-NUMBER:%s",phone);
}
```

The program is designed from the following functions:

1. The function "menu" displays the program menu and receives your option (1, 2, or 3). In this function a **switch** is used to perform different tasks according to the chosen option.

   A. If you choose "1," the file "phones.dat" will be opened for appending (**"a"**). The program will continue accepting data until you respond to the "name" entry by pressing **Enter**, which sends a **NULL** character to the main function.

   B. If you choose "2," the file is opened for reading (**"r"**), and the information is displayed in the shown format.

   C. If you choose "3," the program exits.

2. The function "getinfo" is for data_entry. It accepts the "name" and the "phone" using the macro "ASK." The function returns **NULL** if you skip the first question; otherwise, it returns "DONE" (a constant == 1), which means normal return. Notice that the flag "DONE" is not used in the main function. Any other value can be used as a return value, except the zero (which means **NULL**).

3. The function "write_rec" writes two items (the name and the phone number) to the file using the **fprintf** function and adds a LF character to each string.

4. The function "read_rec" reads two successive lines from the file using the function **fgets**. A check is made for the **EOF** mark using the same function, which returns the value **EOF** if encountered. Otherwise, "DONE" is returned.

5. The function "display_info" displays the "name" and "phone." There is no need for the LF character here as the function **fgets** adds it to each string it reads.

Pay attention to the following points in the program:

1. At the beginning of the main function, a blank line is displayed 24 times. This is a portable method to clear the screen. There is a function to clear the screen with most compilers, but this function, like other graphic functions, is not portable.

2. Note also the alternate method used to define function headers:

```
char getinfo(name, phone)
char name[], phone[];
```

This is the same as:

```
char getinfo(char name[], char phone[])
```

Either one of the two methods is legal with all compilers.

This program uses two simple strings to represent data ("name" and "phone"), but it can be upgraded to support other data items. You may wish to try structures in order to have good control of your data.

DRILL 10-1

Make the necessary modifications to the previous program to let you search for a name instead of displaying the whole file. When you search for a specific name, you may enter only a substring of the name (even one letter). All the names that partially match the input string should be displayed. For example, searching for "ja" will display records of "James," "Jacob," etc. The program must not be case sensitive. You may use the string manipulation tools: **strcmp**, **strlen**, and **strupr**.

10-6 SENDING THE OUTPUT TO THE PRINTER

With most applications you need to get a hardcopy report of the file information. You can use any one of the output functions (**fprintf**, **fputs**, or **putc**) with the stream **stdprn**.

Notice that when you send data to the printer, you must use both the LF character ('\n') and the CR character ('\r') together in order to start printing on the next line. This is not the case when you store data to disk or display them to the screen. This is because the LF character, when written to the disk (in the ASCII files), is translated to a CR and LF pair, but remains LF only in the memory.

DRILL 10-2

Modify the telephone directory to include printing the directory on the printer as a menu option. Your menu could now look something like this:

```
........... MENU ............
1. Add Records to the File.
2. Display File Information.
3. Search for a Record.
4. Hardcopy of Telephone Directory.
5. Exit.
Press the Required Number:
```

10-7 FILING NUMBERS AS STRINGS sprintf

In the last program, you used strings all the way to represent names and phone numbers. When using numeric data, you will need to convert them to strings before you write them to the file. When you read the file, convert the strings back to numbers. A useful function that converts either a **float** or an **int** to a string is the function **sprintf**. The function can be used to handle more than one variable (of any data type) and put them all into one formatted string, padded with the **NULL** character. The function **sprintf** takes the general form:

```
sprintf(s, "format", arg1, arg2,..)
```

where:

       s   is a pointer to the output string.
       format   is the format-characters string.
       arg1,.. are the variables to be converted.

You may use the function **sprintf**, for example, to convert the **float** "salary" to the string "str_salary":

```
sprintf(str_salary, "%f", salary);
```

If "salary" is an **int**, you only change the format character:

```
sprintf(str_salary, "%d", salary);
```

To convert the string back to a number, you can use the conversion functions **atof** or **atoi** as before.

10-8 APPLICATION 2: PAYROLL

Now look at this example in which you store names and wages of employees in the file "wages.dat." The design of the program is similar to that of the "telephone directory" program, except for the following main differences:

1. The file pointer is declared as a local variable and is passed only to those functions which process I/O operations on the file (both methods are legal).

2. Before storing the numeric variable in the file, it is converted to a string using the function **sprintf,** then converted back to a **float** when retrieved from the file.

```
/*   Figure 10-6    */
/* Storing strings and numeric data (floats) in a file */

#include <stdio.h>
#include <math.h>
#include <stdlib.h>
#define MAXSIZE        40+1
#define FNAME          "wages.dat"
#define LF             '\n'
#define DASH           '-'
#define BUFR           80
#define DONE           1
#define ASK(prompt,response)  fputs(prompt,stdout); gets(response)
void menu(void);
void write_rec(char [], float, FILE *);
void file_item(char [], FILE *);
void display_info(char [], float);
void line(void);
/* --------------------    func. main()  -------------------- */
main()
{
    menu();
    return(0);
}
/* -------------------    func. menu    -------------------- */
void menu(void)
{
    FILE *fp;
    static char name[MAXSIZE], option;
    float salary;
    int i;
    for (i=1; i<=24; i++) printf("\n");
    printf(".......... MENU ...........");
    printf("\n\n1. Add Records to the File.");
    printf("\n\n2. Display File Information.");
    printf("\n\n3. Exit.");
    printf("\n\nPress the Required Number:\n");
    option=getch();
    switch(option)
    {
```

```
        case '1':
            fp=fopen(FNAME,"a");
            while (getinfo(name,&salary) != NULL)
               write_rec(name,salary,fp);
            fclose(fp);
            break;
        case '2':
            fp=fopen(FNAME,"r");
            printf("\nNAME\t\t\tSALARY\n\n");
            line();
            while (read_rec(name,&salary,fp) != EOF)
               display_info(name,salary);
            printf("\n\n** End Of File **");
            printf("\nPress any key to continue..\n");
            getch();
            fclose(fp);
            break;
        case '3':
            exit(0);
        default:
            menu();
        }
        menu();
}
/* ----------------- func. getinfo --------------------- */
getinfo(char name[], float *salary)
{
    static char salary_str[MAXSIZE];
    ASK("Enter name:",name);
    if (name[0]==NULL)
       return(NULL);
    ASK("Enter salary:",salary_str);
    *salary = atof(salary_str);
    return(DONE);
}
/* -------------------- func. write_rec ------------------ */
void write_rec(char name[], float salary, FILE *fp)
{
    char strng[MAXSIZE];
    file_item(name,fp);
    sprintf(strng,"%f",salary);
    file_item(strng,fp);
}
/* ----------------- func. file_item ------------------ */
void file_item(char item[], FILE *fp)
{
    int k=0;
    while(item[k] != NULL) {
            putc(item[k],fp);
            k++;
    }
    putc(LF,fp);
}
/* -------------------- func. read_rec --------------------- */
read_rec(char name[], float *salary, FILE *fp)
{
    char rec_strng[MAXSIZE];
    if (fgets(name,BUFR,fp) == NULL)
```

```
        return(EOF);
    if (fgets(rec_strng,BUFR,fp) == NULL)
        return(EOF);
    *salary = atof(rec_strng);
    return(DONE);
}
/* ----------------- func. display_info ------------------- */
void display_info(char name[],float salary)
{
    int i;
    for (i=0;i<=strlen(name);i++)
        if (name[i] != LF)              /* remove LF */
            putc(name[i],stdout);
/* format the numeric field to be left justified at a specific column */
    for (i=1;i<=(32-strlen(name));i++)
        printf(" ");
    printf("$%.2f\n",salary);
}
/* ---------------------- func line ------------------------ */
void line(void)
{
    int i;
    for (i=1;i<=40;i++)
        putc(DASH,stdout) ;
    putc(LF,stdout);
}
```

The following is a sample run of the program:

```
........... MENU ............
1. Add Records to the File.
2. Display File Information.
3. Exit.
Press the Required Number:    ----> Press #2
NAME                          SALARY
------------------------------------------
Tony Penn, Jr.                $1900.34
Tara Strahan                  $2020.40
Jennifer Berlin               $2500.30
** End Of File **
Press any key to continue..
........... MENU ............
1. Add Records to the File.
2. Display File Information.
3. Exit.
Press the Required Number:
```

Some points in this program are worthy of your attention:

1. Because the variables have to be passed by reference (using pointers) to the functions that change their values, the **float** variable was passed to the function "getinfo" using the pointer "&salary." You do not have to do that unless the function is intended to change the contents of the variable.

170

2. If you take a look at the function "display-info," you will notice that the LF character was taken out of the string "name." This is to display the "name" and the "salary" on one line. If you read the file one character at a time, you could do the same thing by stopping before the LF character.

3. Notice also the method used to left-justify the "salary" information in the displayed output using the loop:

```
for (i=1;i<=(32-strlen(name));i++)
    printf(" ");
```

This is an important step because the names are different in length.

4. A new function, "line()," is used here to display a line consisting of 40 dashes, using the constants DASH and LF.

This program can be modified in several ways. For example, you could add the following features:

1. Add the necessary error-check statements to opening and closing files.

2. Modify the program to handle more data items, such as the details of the salary and taxes.

3. Add the necessary statements to protect against erroneous user input.

Good luck.

SUMMARY

> The boldface, in the formulas, represents the keywords and syntax, while the rest is supplied by the programmer. Prototypes of functions are listed in appendix B.

1. You learned in this chapter the main file features of C and became familiar with most of the file handling protocols and tools.

2. You learned how to open and close a file properly, using the following functions:

```
fopen(file_name, access_mode)
fclose(file_pointer)
```

3. You know that there are three essential access modes:

   "r"   **"w"**   **"a"**

   for reading, writing, and appending an ASCII sequential file. You know also that you can modify these modes to allow reading and writing by adding a "+" sign to each:

   "r+"   **"w+"**   **"a+"**

   You know as well that binary files have the following three modes:

   "rb"   **"wb"**   **"ab"**

4. You know how to write data to a file pointed to by a pointer "fp" using the following functions:

   ```
   putc(character, fp)
   fputs(string, fp)
   fprintf(fp, "format", arg1, arg2,...)
   ```

5. You learned how to read back your data items from the file pointed to by the pointer "fp" using the functions:

   ```
   getc(fp)
   fgets(string, number_of_chars, fp)
   ```

6. You learned a new function, **sprintf**, which is useful in creating a formatted string out of one or more variables:

   ```
   sprintf(string, "format", arg1, arg2,..)
   ```

   You used this function to convert a **float** to a string and store it in a file.

7. Finally, during your last tour, you experienced real applications such as the "Telephone Directory" and the "Payroll." Using the tools introduced in this chapter, along with those in the previous chapters, you will be able to do a lot more.

THE NEXT STEP

By the end of day three, you have experienced using the important tools of C that let you create a good application program. However, you may wish to know your position in the C programming world after using this book. As a matter of fact, C is a very rich language. It was born rich, is growing up, and has evolved to **C++** to cope with real-world problems.

You may want to read further about the main topics which are not covered in this book, which are:

- Linked lists
- Unbuffered and Random Access Files
- C graphics (which are compiler dependent)

Other books on C and C++ published by Wordware Publishing, Inc. include *Graphic User Interface Programming with C, Illustrated Borland C++ 3.0, Write Your Own Programming Language Using C++, Object-Oriented Programming Using Turbo C++,* and *Programming Output Drivers Using Borland C++.*

The next step, however, before going to further readings, is to write many programs to practice all that you learned in the three days. Then you will be ready to step from **C** to **C++.**

Appendix A
THE ASCII CHARACTER SET

1. The Printable Characters

Decimal	Octal	Hexadecimal	Character
32	40	20	space
33	41	21	!
34	42	22	"
35	43	23	#
36	44	24	$
37	45	25	%
38	46	26	&
39	47	27	'
40	50	28	(
41	51	29	)
42	52	2a	*
43	53	2b	+
44	54	2c	,
45	55	2d	-
46	56	2e	.
47	57	2f	/
48	60	30	0
49	61	31	1
50	62	32	2
51	63	33	3
52	64	34	4
53	65	35	5
54	66	36	6

Decimal	Octal	Hexadecimal	Character
55	67	37	7
56	70	38	8
57	71	39	9
58	72	3a	:
59	73	3b	;
60	74	3c	<
61	75	3d	=
62	76	3e	>
63	77	3f	?
64	100	40	@
65	101	41	A
66	102	42	B
67	103	43	C
68	104	44	D
69	105	45	E
70	106	46	F
71	107	47	G
72	110	48	H
73	111	49	I
74	112	4a	J
75	113	4b	K
76	114	4c	L
77	115	4d	M
78	116	4e	N
79	117	4f	O
80	120	50	P
81	121	51	Q
82	122	52	R
83	123	53	S
84	124	54	T
85	125	55	U
86	126	56	V
87	127	57	W
88	130	58	X
89	131	59	Y
90	132	5a	Z
91	133	5b	[
92	134	5c	\
93	135	5d	]

Decimal	Octal	Hexadecimal	Character
94	136	5e	^
95	137	5f	_
96	140	60	`
97	141	61	a
98	142	62	b
99	143	63	c
100	144	64	d
101	145	65	e
102	146	66	f
103	147	67	g
104	150	68	h
105	151	69	i
106	152	6a	j
107	153	6b	k
108	154	6c	l
109	155	6d	m
110	156	6e	n
111	157	6f	o
112	160	70	p
113	161	71	q
114	162	72	r
115	163	73	s
116	164	74	t
117	165	75	u
118	166	76	v
119	167	77	w
120	170	78	x
121	171	79	y
122	172	7a	z
123	173	7b	{
124	174	7c		
125	175	7d	}
126	176	7e	~

2. The Punctuation Characters

Decimal	Octal	Hexadecimal	Character
33	41	21	!
34	42	22	"
35	43	23	#
36	44	24	$
37	45	25	%
38	46	26	&
39	47	27	'
40	50	28	(
41	51	29	)
42	52	2a	*
43	53	2b	+
44	54	2c	,
45	55	2d	-
46	56	2e	.
47	57	2f	/
58	72	3a	:
59	73	3b	;
60	74	3c	<
61	75	3d	=
62	76	3e	>
63	77	3f	?
64	100	40	@
91	133	5b	[
92	134	5c	\
93	135	5d	]
94	136	5e	^
95	137	5f	_
96	140	60	`
123	173	7b	{
124	174	7c	|
125	175	7d	}
126	176	7e	~

3. The Control Characters

Decimal	Octal	Hexadecimal	Key	Backslash Code	Mnemonic Code
0	0	0	^@	'\0'	NUL
1	1	1	^A		SOH
2	2	2	^B		STX
3	3	3	^C		ETX
4	4	4	^D		EOT
5	5	5	^E		ENQ
6	6	6	^F		ACK
7	7	7	^G	'\a'	BEL
8	10	8	^H	'\b'	BS
9	11	9	^I	'\t'	HT
10	12	a	^J	'\n'	LF
11	13	b	^K	'\v'	VT
12	14	c	^L	'\f'	FF
13	15	d	^M	'\r'	CR
14	16	e	^N		SO
15	17	f	^O		SI
16	20	10	^P		DLE
17	21	11	^Q		DC1
18	22	12	^R		DC2
19	23	13	^S		DC3
20	24	14	^T		DC4
21	25	15	^U		NAK
22	26	16	^V		SYN
23	27	17	^W		ETB
24	30	18	^X		CAN
25	31	19	^Y		EM
26	32	1a	^Z		SUB
27	33	1b	ESC		ESC
28	34	1c			FS
29	35	1d			GS
30	36	1e			RS
31	37	1f			US
127	177	7f	DEL		DEL

Appendix B

PROTOTYPES OF FUNCTIONS
(discussed in this book)

1. I/O FUNCTIONS:

int fclose(FILE *fp)	stdio.h
char *fgets(char *string, int number_of_chars, FILE *fp)	stdio.h
FILE *fopen(char *file_name, char *access_mode)	stdio.h
int fprintf(FILE *fp, char *format, arg1, arg2, ...)	stdio.h
int fputs(char *string, FILE *fp)	stdio.h
int getc(FILE *fp)	stdio.h
int getch(void)	conio.h
int getchar(void)	stdio.h
int getche(void)	conio.h
char *gets(char *string)	stdio.h
int printf(char *format, arg1, arg2, ...)	stdio.h
int putc(int character, FILE *fp)	stdio.h
int putchar(int character)	stdio.h
int puts(char *string)	stdio.h
int scanf(char *format, arg1, arg2, ...)	stdio.h
int sprintf(char *string, char *format, arg1, arg2, ...)	stdio.h

2. STRING MANIPULATION FUNCTIONS:

char *strcat(char *string1, char *string2)	string.h
char *strchr(char *string, int character)	string.h
int strcmp(char *string1, char *string2)	string.h
char *strcpy(char *string1, char *string2)	string.h
unsigned strlen(char *string)	string.h
char *strlwr(char *string)	string.h
char *strncpy(char *string1, char *string2, int count)	string.h
char *strupr(char *string)	string.h

3. CHARACTER MANIPULATION AND TESTING FUNCTIONS:

int isalnum(int character)	ctype.h
int isalpha(int character)	ctype.h
int isascii(int character)	ctype.h
int iscntrl(int character)	ctype.h
int isdigit(int character)	ctype.h
int isgraph(int character)	ctype.h
int islower(int character)	ctype.h
int isprint(int character)	ctype.h
int ispunct(int character)	ctype.h
int isspace(int character)	ctype.h
int isupper(int character)	ctype.h
int isxdigit(int character)	ctype.h
int tolower(int character)	ctype.h
	Quick C: redefined in stdlib.h
int toupper(int character)	ctype.h
	Quick C: redefined in stdlib.h

4. TYPE CONVERSION FUNCTIONS:

double atof(char *string)	stdlib.h, math.h
int atoi(char *string)	stdlib.h
long atol(char *string)	stdlib.h
char *itoa(int number, char *string, int radix)	stdlib.h
char *ltoa(long number, char *string, int radix)	stdlib.h

5. MISCELLANEOUS FUNCTIONS:

void exit(int number**)**	**stdlib.h**
int kbhit(void)	**conio.h**
void *malloc(unsigned number_of_bytes**)**	**stdlib.h**
	Turbo C: **stdlib.h, alloc.h**
	Quick C: **stdlib.h, malloc.h**
double pow(double base**, double** exponent**)**	**math.h**
int system(char *DOS_command_string**)**	**stdlib.h**

Index